The Power
of Etiquette

Essentials to Building
Rewarding Relationships with
onfiden   Grace

©2022 Pipe Publishing

The Power of Etiquette
Essentials to Building Rewarding Relationships with Confidence and Grace

Pipe Publishing
Fort Pierce, FL

ISBN 978-1-5136-9126-8

Library of Congress Cataloging-in-Publication data is available.
Etiquette/
Printed in the United States
First Edition

CONTENTS

Good manners have much to do
with the emotions.
To make them ring true, one must
feel them, not merely exhibit them.

Amy Vanderbilt

FOREWORD

The Power of Etiquette

Dr. Larthenia Howard

Most of my preteen and teenage years I was sort of a "tomboy". I played football in the streets with the boys, was the only girl in the county's baseball league, and thought it was cool to detest wearing dresses while sporting the same pair of Levi jeans to school at least twice a week. It wasn't that my parents could not afford clothing for me, quite the opposite. However, as a growing girl and best friend of my male cousin who was about the same age, I thought it was hipper to hang with the boys and thereby took on some of their less than pleasant hygiene ways. My parents were agricultural farmers, so dirt and grime were familiar. I often worked the fields and had no quorums waddling with Mother Nature.

It was my 8th grade year when my grandmother finally had enough of my "tomboyish" ways and insisted I attend an afterschool program designed to teach girls how to be young ladies. This was my first encounter with etiquette. I wanted nothing to do with what I imagined as the prissy, stuffy stuff. However, it wasn't long into the program that the course material piqued my interest. This was new territory. I was fascinated by the idea that there is protocol for many of the everyday encounters we have with one another.

After that 8th grade season, years would pass before the topic of etiquette resurfaced in my circle. And recently, many years later I met Cheryl, an etiquette and protocol expert. We worked together to create her first solo author project and the topic was—you guessed it, etiquette. Like so many years ago, I was fascinated by the topic. The intricate details of what to do, what not to do, and how to do what is proper when interacting with others was quite intriguing. You see, etiquette is about more than engaging properly and appropriately. Time with Cheryl taught me that etiquette is about relationship, reputation, and respect.

In short, relationships are impacted by our behaviors and how we communicate. Knowing proper etiquette can influence making a deal or breaking a deal because your brand is reflected in how others view you. That's important. That ma   power.

                              is a collection of five experts in the field.
                    s of experiences in training and teaching
                    and protocol. They share their insights in
                    asy to grasp and apply. My hope is that

The Power of Etiquette is influential in better understanding how to use the concepts to raise the bar of excellence in your everyday dealings. Done well, the ideas shared here separate you from the masses. They have certainly been instrumental in how I engage others in different areas of life, including dining, written communication, networking, leadership development, and other topics.

Included in this anthology are several QR codes. Hover your smartphone's camera over the code and enjoy a video of additional material. Too, each author has inserted Power Tips at the end their chapter. Power Tips are brief take-aways designed to prompt quick action. Our hope is that you consciously consider how to better engage etiquette in all your interactions.

RENITA JACKSON

Renita Jackson loves and lives in her native hometown of St. Louis, Missouri. She is a graduate of Southern Illinois University at Edwardsville where she earned her BS Degree in Mass Communications and Public Relations. She worked several years in radio broadcasting and in the insurance industry. She received her etiquette training and certification in 2004 at The Etiquette Institute.

That same year, Renita founded Jackson Etiquette, LLC., however, her passion for etiquette and doing things the proper way goes back much further. As a little girl growing up in St. Louis, Renita's mother taught her sister, brother and her, the different aspects of etiquette and manners simply by consulting an etiquette reference book they had in their home. The lessons instilled by their mom continue to be a passion of Renita's today.

In addition to her membership with The Etiquette Institute, Renita has affiliations with The Protocol School of Washington and the National Association of Urban Etiquette Professionals.

Renita is married and is the proud mother of two handsome sons, one beautiful stepdaughter and four wonderful grandchildren. She is an active member at Church On The Rock, where she serves with the Host Ministry Team and is a Youth Leader for the Uprising Youth Ministry.

Renita teaches etiquette classes and social skills workshops to children and adults in public and private schools, universities, community organizations, businesses, and various other organizations. Renita is the author of "Everyone Could Use a Little More Etiquette," a book on business & social etiquette and everyday manners.

1

GREETINGS AND INTRODUCTIONS

Don't Just Stand There, Introduce Yourself!

Renita Jackson

There is no accomplishment so
easy to acquire as politeness
and none more profitable.

George Bernard Shaw

It is true; you never have a second chance to make a first impression. Do it right the first time. It takes only a few seconds to make a good impression. It can take a lifetime to eliminate a poor one. You are the director of your own first impression.

Many people find they have trouble with meeting other people. Do not sweat it. Be it a business meeting or a social setting, making introductions, starting conversations or networking introductions can present some awkward situations. Good first impressions do really matter. They can make or break a business deal, determine the direction of a relationship, grant you the needed respect in a volunteer or leadership position, or maybe place you in the catalog of other forgotten people. Make a successful start with the proper introduction. Follow these six steps to make quality, lasting impressions.

Six steps of an introduction

Stand – Stand up during an introduction. Unless you have some type of impairment that might cause you difficulty, you should stand. It is not only a professional thing to do, but also a courteous gesture that shows respect to the other person. It also lets the other person know you have a sincere desire to meet them. Gender has no rank here, both men and women should stand during the introduction. It used to be in a more social setting women had the option to remain seated when being introduced to a man. This has changed. Both men and women stand for introductions for all occasions. If you are dining at a table, it is not necessary to stand for the introduction.

Children should stand when being introduced to adults. Elderly people and people with disabilities may have difficulties standing and are not expected to do so.

Smile – It improves your face value! You may have heard the adage that it takes fewer muscles to smile than it does to frown. Well, I am not sure if that is true but keep smiling so you do not have to work so hard! A smile is a universal language. You may be wearing a designer dress or a custom-tailored suit, but a warm smile is a valuable and positive feature that will add volumes to your appearance. It lets others know you are friendly. Who wants to meet a grumpy person anyway?

Make Eye Contact – Have you ever been in a conversation with someone who would not maintain eye contact with you while talking? It is quite distracting. You wonder, "What are they looking at?" Avoid looking down at the floor or the scenery behind the person. Look people in their eyes during an introduction and when holding a conversation with them. It gives you confidence and it makes them feel special. Some people are challenged with low self-esteem in this area. If you need help try this tip; when talking with someone, look at the bridge of the person's nose right between their eyes. Due to the proximity, no one can tell if you are not looking them in the eyes. Eventually your confidence will grow, and you will be able to look directly into the eyes of others.

Shake Hands – Simply put, it shows very good manners if you shake hands with the person you are meeting. Shake with your right hand, which is acceptable by most cultures globally, even if you're lefthanded. Shake for approximately 2-3 seconds or 2 up and down hand pumps. No wimpy, wilted fish handshakes and no bone-crushing ones either! If you tend to have clammy hands, dry them before you shake someone's hand. Keep a handkerchief or tissue in your hand for a quick dry-off before a handshake. No one wants to shake a wet hand. This step is gender equal too. Both men and women shake hands.

If someone is in the process of dining when you meet him or her, you may not want to shake their hand, as he or she may find it necessary but inconvenient to wash their hands again to continue with the meal. Do not shake hands with others if you have a cold or if your hands are dirty for some reason. Offer your apologies for not shaking hands with him or her. You can simply say, "Please forgive me for not shaking your hand, but I don't want to pass germs from my cold." If you meet a person who has a disability with his or her right hand, follow their lead. If he or she extends his or her left hand for the handshake, you follow with the same.

A handshake when departing a casual meeting or conversation is an optional choice. It is not necessary, but it is a nice gesture.

Say Your Name – Hello! My name is _____. Say both your first and last names clearly. If you have an honorific or title such as Dr. or Mrs. or a designation such as Ph.D., M.D., or Esq., do not use it while making general introductions. Just give your name. You may use the honorific if it is necessary in the introduction, such as a doctor meeting a patient's family for the first time.

Repeat Their Name – When introduced, repeat the person's name to make sure you are pronouncing it correctly. It also helps you to remember their name and it makes the other person feel good. If you forget a person's name, simply apologize, and ask him or her to repeat their name again for you. By the way, if someone pronounces your name incorrectly, kindly correct them. No harm done.

Introducing others

Many people are very uncomfortable with this. Introducing yourself to someone is easy, you know yourself better than anyone else does. However, what should you do if you are with a friend and another person joins you? In a situation like this, an introduction will make everyone feel comfortable and invited to join the conversation. How do you handle making proper introductions with others? It is simple; the most important thing to remember about introducing others is to do it. Do not just stand there without saying anything. That makes everyone feel a little uneasy. Even if you have forgotten someone's name or you do not make the introduction perfectly, that is okay—at least you tried. There are no etiquette police ready to issue a citation if you get it wrong. Give it your best effort. It makes people feel important when they are introduced to others.

Another important thing to remember when introducing others is to always begin the introduction by saying the name of the person of person of honor first, then the rest of the introduction will fall into place. Who is the honored person?

- Authority over lessor authority:
  "Dr. Ryan Royce, I'd like you to meet George Drew and Lorraine Roberts."

- Older over younger:
  "Grandma, this is my friend Regina Roberts."

- Female over male:
  "Gwen Jackson please meet LeRoy Banks."

Always tell how you know the person you are introducing. People being introduced should remember to use the six steps of the introduction. People being introduce should add a nice pleasantly such as, "It's nice to meet you."

The fundamental purpose of precedence is to determine who or what goes first and is of great importance to many people, especially those of rank and authority. This can carry over to other things such as office locations, dinner or meeting seating, flag placements and more. It is also an important part of introducing other people. While it may not be readily recognizable in most everyday meetings of people, it is still a good thing to know, because you never know when you may need to make such an introduction.

Social distancing

In 2020 the universe was faced with a challenge most had never experienced in their lifetime. COVID-19, also known as the Coronavirus, caused a shutdown to our lifestyle and the way we normally do things. As people began to wear masks, stay six feet apart, slather hand sanitizer and do most everything virtually, we experienced a *new normal*—a different way of doing things for everyone's safety. One of the frequent used terms coming out of the new normal was, *social distancing*. Personally, I believed social distancing was not an option, as we must always remain social. Physical distancing is more of what was appropriate at the time.

With the physical distancing, the handshake took a backseat and alternatives to meeting people were put into action. The fist-bump, elbow bump and even for a short time, the foot bump were the inventive substitutes to the handshake. During this time, these options were creative ways to keep people communicating, but they were never meant to replace the customary and universal greeting of the handshake.

⚘ POWER TIPS ⚘

Tips for making introductions:

- Good introductions help to make positive first impressions. Practice this skill to build your confidence and be prepared when meeting others.

- Occasionally you will forget someone's name, that's okay. . . simply asked for it again, repeat it out loud one time, but several times in your mind to make a better mental block of it in your head.

- Unless necessary for the occasion, do not use abbreviations and honorifics when introducing yourself, but use them when introducing others or addressing them.

- Say the name of the more honored person first and the rest of the introduction will fall into place.

- A poor introduction is better than none.

Send out a cheerful, postive greeting,
and most of the time you will get back
a cheerful, positive greeting.
It's also true if you send out a negative
greeting, you will, in most cases,
get back a negative greeting.

Zig Ziglar

✎ TRUDY SNAITH ✎

An Internationally certified Etiquette, Corporate Protocol consultant and educator, trained at The Protocol School of Washington, The American School of Etiquette, and Institut Villa Pierrefeu (Switzerland), Trudy instructs youth, corporate clients and individuals registered in programs offered by her school.

Founder of The Executive School of Protocol, she is also CEO and serves on the Board of Directors; She is the Principal of Institut International, Bermuda, developing residential and summer programs for teens and mature young ladies. Etiquette consultant for the Kardias Club Debutante Program under which she created the Pillars of Philanthropy© program. A philanthropy education program piloted in 2015 that prepared senior school students for roles as future philanthropists or facilitators of philanthropy. It graduated its first class in July 2016.

Trudy is a published author of *Bermuda Shorts and More: Bermudian Lifestyle, Etiquette and Culture* and, the *Bermudian Girl* series of historical fiction for children. She is also the creator and host of the *Sarah Catherine Tea for Young Ladies* held annually in the

St. George's Historical Society Garden and attended by many delighted girls. Among her accomplishments is the founding of Bermuda's first classical music store *Opus Encore*, that served the musical needs of Bermuda schools, The Bermuda Festival of Performing Arts, and the public.

Community activities include serving as President of the International Women's Forum Bermuda from September 2017 to October 2019; Former Board of Trustees of the Bermuda High School for Girls; and Executive chairman of KTMC Ltd. She also sits on the advisory committee of The St. George's Historical Society. In 2015, she piloted the philanthropy education program (Pillars of Philanthropy©), an intensive nine-month program that prepared senior school students for roles as future philanthropists or facilitators of philanthropy, graduating its first class in July 2016.

Though semi-retired, she will still conduct classes in etiquette and afternoon tea on demand. She also continues to write books. Her husband Kenneth is a retired Dental Surgeon. They have two lovely, successful adult children and four grandchildren also living in Bermuda.

tsnaith@gmail.com
www.esop.bm
www.bermudiangirl.bm

2

THE WRITTEN WORD AS AN ART FORM

Trudy Snaith

Manners are like the shadows of virtues—
they are the momentary display of
those qualities which our fellow
creatures love and respect.

Sydney Smith

Writing or recording one's thoughts and sentiments on something permanent is an age-old form of communication. To develop an appreciation for the beauty of it all is not only simple, but beneficial as well. Composing a handwritten letter or note is a form of meditation that requires that one slows down and reflects carefully on the words to be used. And what can be more delightful than to receive a beautifully addressed envelope containing a letter to be read at one's leisure, perhaps with a cup of tea or glass of wine.

Etiquette teaches why you should write as well as the construction basics of thank you notes, business and social letters, invitations, and more. I will not address those things here. Instead, I share with you the pleasures that can be found through letter writing and the benefit of the etiquette enhanced lifestyle it creates. Putting together a basic 'stationary wardrobe' that is built on its functionality and an appreciation for the beauty of its contents, signals that one is aware of its importance. The pleasure you find in using this stationary wardrobe, accentuated by your personal touch, is a bonus. It becomes part of establishing the etiquette lifestyle that makes it easier to cope with the stresses of today's world.

The visual simulation of beautifully created paper and cards is difficult to resist, and one longs to share that with special friends. It is a highly satisfying experience.

Many people have said to me that their penmanship is not to their liking and that's why they do not write letters. Good penmanship takes practice. But in the meantime, the appearance of what is written can be improved by a few simple preparations that give pleasing results. A ruler, a no. 2 pencil (or any pencil that writes faintly) and an eraser are your go to tools. After the ink is thoroughly dry, the pencil marks can be erased, and no one is the wiser. Your correspondence looks beautiful.

The absolute best reference book for stationary is *Crane's Blue Book of Stationary* by Steven L. Feinberg.

Amusing historical tidbit

Calling cards were very popular years ago and I think they could be quite useful still in today's modern world. About the size of a standard business card, they were generally used to announce the caller, or the name of the person making the visit. Only the name of the caller should be on the card. And according to *Manners, Etiquette, and Deportment of the Most Refined Society*, by John H. Young, published in 1879, they *'Can convey a subtle and unmistakable intelligence. It's texture, style of engraving and even the hour of leaving it combine to place the stranger whose name it bears, in a pleasant or disagreeable attitude, even before his manners, conversation and face have been able to explain his social position,'* The author also states that a corner of the card was to be turned down, indicating if the card was left in person or folded in half if left for the lady of the house.

A calling card should be left for each adult you are calling upon. There are many rules about how many cards you are permitted to leave and who exactly (male or female) is leaving the card. The size is even restricted by who is leaving the card—single or married woman, a male, a married couple and even a child. Goodness, how did one keep up? And of course, there were strict rules about how the name of the person presenting the card was written on it.

With the current availability of numerous printing options many people have business cards used in the same way calling cards were used years ago. Typical business cards contain a lot more information about an individual than calling cards.

A reference book I've found valuable in understanding how intricate the rules of correspondence were at that time is the *Encyclopedia of Etiquette: A Book of Manners for Everyday Use*, by Emily Holt, originally published in 1921.

Personal stationary

The purpose of a stationary wardrobe is to have ready on hand, stationary for any occasion. You are not restricted by the inconvenience of having to dash out to a store when you feel the need to engage in written correspondence.

I advise that the core of a basic stationary wardrobe should consist of the traditionally recommended contents, of the best quality you can afford. Stationary that reflects your personality and style are personal choices that can be added later. The creation of your stationary wardrobe is rewarding in that it generates the satisfaction that comes from an appreciation for beauty and the finer things in life. It also gives you an opportunity to reflect and express your creativity with words.

Listed here are the contents of a basic stationary wardrobe. My personal stationary wardrobe begins with these items and is then expanded by an assortment of paper sizes and other essentials.

- Letter sheets

Letter sheets are the most formal piece of writing paper in the wardrobe. It is a sheet of paper, 8 ½ by 11 inches, folded in half along the left side. When the letter is completed, it is again folded in half and placed in an envelope. Following is the correct sequence of writing on a folded letter sheet. You would write on page one, page three and then page two. Page one of the folded sheet is the page facing you. Page two is the page on the left side when you open the folded letter sheet. Page three is the page on the right that is across from page two. Letter sheets are also single sheets of paper the same size as a folded letter sheet. It is acceptable with letter sheets, to have a monogram centered at the top of the first page. Suitable to be used for any type of correspondence. There is a difference in size between US letter paper and A4 (some companies refer to their stationary sizes beginning with letters of the alphabet) paper sheets. The important thing here is to be certain you buy envelopes that go with the stationary you have selected.

- Monogrammed notes. 4.25 x 5.5 cards, when folded in half.

- Correspondence cards (my favorite) 15 x 11 cm (5.9 in x 4.33). Useful for any type of correspondence from thank you notes to invitations or just general correspondence. The choices are many. There are plain cards with simple borders, or cards with decorative edgings. Having an assortment of correspondence cards on hand allows you to be prepared for any occasion.

- House stationary: Stationary with the house name monogramed or engraved on it. Typically, the house name is found at the top center but can be in other areas of the stationary chosen. For social business communication, I use correspondence cards with 'The Executive School of Protocol' centered at the top. A good stationary store will assist you with making decisions in this process.

- Envelopes: If envelopes are not included with your stationary, always be certain you buy the correct matching size. I live in a humid climate and share with you a tip that has served me well over the years. I cut small rectangles of wax paper to place under the flap of newly purchased envelopes before storing them away. Thus, I avoid the disappointment of discovering my envelopes are stuck together when I am ready to use them. This has served me well no matter how many years have elapsed.

- Mailing stamps: It's good to have stamps available for local letters in your stationary wardrobe. Letters mailed to foreign addresses will have to be weighed by the post office.

- Though not considered part of a stationary wardrobe, I include several journals in mine. Leather bound journals are a beautiful addition and ideal for recording daily life and practicing handwriting.

In addition to quality stationary that you purchase, stationary acquired during travel can add an interesting dimension to your collection when used selectively in my opinion. Friends in my travel groups who have often visited the same places appreciate reminders that the stationary elicits. It opens the way to pleasant conversation of past shared experiences. Top end hotels and other organizations often make available attractive stationary for their patrons. Though it may be the company letterhead and not your own, it is hard to resist adding stationary with something like the Venice-Simplon Orient Express at the top when offered to you. Especially when upon your arrival you find that the company has added your name to the stationary just under their own letterhead.

Remembering the statement from the 1879 etiquette book. "*Stationary can convey a subtle and unmistakable intelligence. Making favorable and lasting impressions, in the absence of the writer's physical presence, is always advantageous.*"

Stationary paper can be purchased from numerous places. And many styles are fun to have and send. But your personal stationary wardrobe should always have as it's foundation the traditional, basic pieces for those occasions that will call for it. The quality of the paper you chose is very important so do not skimp there. The paper is always unruled. Some find it fashionable to choose colors that indicate their personal flair for the dramatic and that may be fine for certain occasions. But the colors for a woman's traditional, basic personal social stationary, should be buff or other soft colors. These are considered classier and have always been an indication of good taste. Jacqueline Onassis Kennedy was known for her favoring of soft blue colored stationary.

Classic sources of stationary

Crane: https://www.crane.com/
Smythson: https://www.smythson.com/us/stationery
Leeming Brothers: https://leemingbrothers.co.uk/
The Wren Press: https://wrenpress.co.uk/

The Social stationary wardrobe for men adds plain white as a color option along with buff or light grey.

- Monarch

- Half sheets

- Correspondence cards

- Envelopes

- Stamps

Business and professional stationary

Not considered part of a personal social stationary wardrobe, business stationary is always plain white, unruled and $8\frac{1}{2}$ by 11" sheets with the Corporate Letterhead at the top. As a standard, conservative color inks such as black and grey should be used. However, this could change based on the type of business the letter is coming from.

Addressing envelopes and other basics

A ruler and no. 2 pencil should be used to draw very light lines on the paper (and envelope) to write your message. Once completed and the ink is dry, these lines should be erased. The envelope is the first impression, and it should be as perfect as you can manage. Do not be shy about writing out the name and address faintly in pencil. If you don't like the way it looks, it can be erased. When you are satisfied, then trace over that with the fountain pen.

The name of the recipient is centered on the front of the envelope. The first address line follows below on the next line aligned to the left. Additional address lines follow the same pattern. The return address for business letters is written in the top left corner of the front of the envelope. Return address for personal letters is centered at the top of the back of the envelope. Only the address is required if placed on the back of the envelope—no name.

Tips and extras that set one apart from average

Fountain Pens: I believe that every serious writer of letters should own a fountain pen. A fountain pen makes an elegant impression and is always distinguishable from ballpoint or roller ball pen writing. There are many fountain pens in my collection. I have standards like Mont Blanc, Lamy, Parker, Waterman, and others. I collect fountain pens whenever I travel because they are so pretty. I even have a Mont Blanc calligraphy tip fountain pen that the company sold in the mid 70's and is no longer produced. A good example of the reason to not put off buying something you admire.

Some fountain pens take cartridges and others take ink drawn up from a bottle. When purchasing bottled ink, be sure to use the correct ink for your pen. There is a difference between fountain pen ink and calligraphy pen ink. Calligraphy pen ink is thicker and will clog a fountain pen. If filling the pen from a bottle, 'bleed' or discard about three drops out before starting to write. Place the cap on the end of the pen when writing, it gives the pen the correct weight it needs to be properly balanced.

Lastly, it is important to allow all ink to dry thoroughly before doing anything else to the letter or envelope.

Interesting fountain pen sites:

(http://www.richardspens.com/index.html)
(https://www.artofmanliness.com/articles/a-primer-on-fountain-pens/)

Additional accessories:

In keeping with the creation of environments that embrace the etiquette enhanced lifestyle we wish to achieve; we recognize that beautiful accessories can complement the pleasures of the writing experience.

Inkwells: Are attractive desk accessories. You can find about anything online these days but for those who enjoy browsing, some stationary stores carry them. Antique shops and flea markets are other potentially good sources for glass inkwells.

Stationary box: The wooden box pictured here is from the Crane stationary company. It appears that the Crane company no longer sells them. The only place I was able to find a similar Crane stationary box was on Amazon. I did come across an interesting site, the Galen Leather Company (https://www.galenleather.com/products/the-writing-box), that had nice looking wooden stationary boxes.

I have decorated cigar boxes to make stationary boxes as gifts for young people. Having their own stationary box is a simple effective way to get them interested in writing letters and notes. Another source of a fabulous looking stationary box, can be seen by following the British stationary company Smythson's link (https://www.smythson.com/us/navy-mara-stationery-bureau-1025592.html?cgid=524) for those who really want to splurge. I am certain though, there are many other sources of wooden stationary boxes that can be found by a Google search.

Sealing wax: Sealing wax has been used for centuries. First used to signify the authenticity of the writer, and later to confirm the letter had not been opened until received by the intended recipient. These days a letter with a wax seal on the back of an envelope adds a bit of elegance and personal distinction to the letter you have written. The gold used to enhance the wax stamp once placed on the envelope is called gold cream. It is also available in silver.

My sealing wax preference is the stick type, but I know it is also available in pellet form that you melt in a small bowl over a heat source then pour onto your envelope. I have also seen sealing wax that comes in glue gun type devices. This would be an advantage if you are applying sealing wax to a lot of envelopes. There are multiple sources of sealing waxes. Here is a link that will take you to a good history of sealing wax and how to use it:

(https://www.artofmanliness.com/articles/wax-seals-a-history-and-how-to/)

Wax burner: I discovered the lovely wax burner pictured, from Bartolutti, (https://bortoletti.com/) after many years of burning my fingertips. The company is a wonderful Italian supplier of calligraphy pens, calligraphy ink, sealing wax, sealing wax stamps and other quality stationary products. Their customer service is excellent, and they deliver worldwide.

Wax Seal Application

Sealing wax stamps: There are so many choices for this. Most people begin with a stamp of their initials. A family signet ring can also be used as a stamp. There are companies that will design and create a wax stamp especially for you. And once again, you can find unusual wax stamps during your travels. In my collection, I have a jade wax stamp I picked up in Hong Kong. I was told the inscription means 'good luck.' I fell in love with the blue Murano glass stamp from Venice when I discovered Bartoletti. The metal portion (or initial / design) part of the sealing wax stamp is usually interchangeable so it's a good idea when ordering your stamp to see the different replacement stamp options that are available. This link will give you an idea of typical designs that are available (https://bortoletti.com/product-category/wax-seal-stamp/bronze-initials-simbols/).

The Executive School of Protocol website is being updated and under construction. Please feel free to contact me by email: tsnaith@gmail.com

❧ POWER TIPS ❧

- Creating a stationary wardrobe is a pleasurable and rewarding experience, not to be rushed.

- Choose items to include in your stationary wardrobe things that reflect your personality, what you wish to express to individuals who will receive letters and cards you send them.

- Also choose things that will create a pleasurable experience for you as you use them. Appreciating the beauty of fine crafted items to include in your stationary wardrobe will help to set an atmosphere that generates the flow of words when writing letters.

- If by chance you are tempted to write a letter in anger - never send it right away. Wait a day or two to reread what you have written. After you have cooled down the letter usually takes on a different meaning and you'll find it wiser to discard it.

- Always choose the best quality of products you can afford. You will appreciate them more and the distinction is noticeable.

- Don't stress if you don't have perfect penmanship. That can easily be improved with practice.

- A letter written with warm, genuine sentiments always leaves a lasting impression. Enjoy the process.

✑ CHERYL WALKER-ROBERTSON ∿

Cheryl Walker-Robertson is a certified international protocol professional, an Author, Moderator, Facilitator, Trainer, and a Coach. She is often referred to as the 'Protocol Ambassador'.

As the Founder and CEO of Protocol International, a professional behavior, and interpersonal skills development consulting firm, she is dedicated to helping executives, entrepreneurs and aspiring professionals enhance their soft diplomacy skills, and improve their personal brand. For more than two decades Protocol International has designed and implemented communication and leadership training programs, moderated panels, activated tours, and served as brand ambassador. Some of her clients include Prudential, PepsiCo, US Embassy, Viacom, US Department of Commerce, Intercontinental Hotels, AmeriHealth Caritas, Publicis, Barclays Bank, Keystone First and The Ritz Carlton, to name a few.

Walker-Robertson has helped her clients learn to be more confident, courteous, and strategic in business and in social situations. Individuals and groups that embrace Protocol International programs represent business, government, education, sports and entertainment. Considered a thought leader in her field Ms. Walker-Robertson is a contributing writer to various international trade and business publications and is frequently the protocol expert for several organizations, blogs, podcasts, webinars and appears frequently on podcasts and news programs.

Ms. Walker-Robertson, born and raised in Philadelphia, Pennsylvania studied under the direction of Dorothea Johnson, Protocol Advisor and Liaison to the Washington Diplomatic Community for the Joint Military Attaché'. She earned a BS in Business Management from St. Augustine's University, an associate degree in Liberal Arts from Harcum College, a Certificate in Management from Penn State Executive Development Program, a Certificate in Negotiation from University of Notre Dame and is Certified by Berlitz International as a licensed practitioner in cultural competence awareness as a Cultural Navigator. She has been an executive in the corporate arena for over 20 years in Sales and Marketing, a member of the International Association of Protocol Officers, International Association of Image Consultants, National Chamber of Commerce, National Association of Professional Women and the Association of Sales Training and Development, Society for Human Resources, and Women in Sports and Entertainment.

She is the best-selling author of "Rules of Engagement" How To Win at Dining with Clients and other Important People", Co-author of "The Power of Civility, the Secrets of Social Capital" and upcoming "Power of Etiquette, The Essentials of Building Rewarding Relationships with Confidence and Grace".

3

NETWORKING: THE ULTIMATE POWER TOOL

Cheryl Walker-Robertson

Every action done in company ought to be with some sign of respect to those that are present.

George Washington, Rules of Civility and Decent Behavior

Have you ever been to a networking session where someone passes out their business cards like Mrs. Fields cookies? Perhaps you have been in the company of someone in a networking meeting and instead of giving you great eye contact they keep eyeing the door. How about the person you just friended on Facebook and now you are notified about everything they do, hear, think, play, and eat? There are wrong ways to network and there are ways to network that demonstrate a culture of civility. The networking we are presenting in this chapter, in a book whose focus is on civility, is about inspiring people and building long term relationships as a result of having civility when networking.

Networking, the noun, is people talking to each other, sharing ideas, information, and resources. Networking, the verb, is what happens when there is a planned event or gathering with the primary goal of connecting with others. The verb is an action word with a fundamental focus on meeting people, and having people meet you. It's what you do and how you do what you do to make people comfortable with and engaged by you. This does not discount the networking that happens in the parking lot, in the supermarket, in the bank and at the car wash—all equally important opportunities to demonstrate civility during a human moment.

For the purposes of this chapter, we are discussing strategies on "working a room", the art of mingling with civility, its beauty, and benefits.

The benefits of networking with civility include...

- Giving and getting (in that order) that builds rapport with people.
- Sharing contacts and resources that makes solidifies you are a resource and have a resource.
- Trying out thoughts and ideas.

The beauty of networking with civility…

- Members of your network ensure that you are informed on all things relevant to you i.e., you get a call from the meeting with an update.

- Your associates reach out to you with a referral and/or an email when they meet someone that you should know i.e., you get an email introduction or recommendation.

- You have a level of trust that leaves confidential information confidential and get advice that is invaluable and genuine i.e., run a business idea by a colleague who gives you an extra added value, building on your idea making it even better.

Networking is an invaluable tool that everyone should utilize, and businessmen and women should master. Adding the dynamic of networking with civility is the icing on the cake. The adage says it's not what you know but who you know. I'd like to add, it's also who they know and how well you treat them all.

Another cliché is people do business with people they like. Again, I'd like to add, people do business with people they feel comfortable with and who abide by the same rules and the same civilities. It makes them all members of the same club—automatic trust.

Successful people possess highly refined networking skills and a sense of civility in their interaction that is unmistakable. You've seen that person- she seems like she knows everyone in the room and everyone in the room seems to know her. She has a comfort level and confidence that benefits not only her but the host of the event as well and everyone she interacts with. Her demonstration of civility brings a sense of ease to everyone in the room. Her influence makes a positive shift in the ambience of the room and the event. What host or hostess is not grateful for what someone like that brings to the table? These master networkers are always invited, and they approach networking prepared, poised, and considerate. The central principle of networking at this level of excellence is one of civility; the concept of giving includes the universal reward for giving which is getting.

Every author in this book is an expert sharing ordinary concepts that with civility will get extraordinary results. Behaving with civility is the ultimate networking tool. Great networking with the added value of civility is both a skill set and a character trait. Both of which can be acquired. This life strategy is empowering and will give you the confidence to thrive at business functions, in networking situations, in relationships and in life. Not having your networking skills up to par can mean lost opportunities and contacts. The key to networking civility is taking the initiative, being a giver, and constantly working on refining important relationships. I am pleased to present to you Top Ten Tips for Networking with Civility. Please consider the following:

1. **RSVP- the civility of confirmation**

   Too often hosts find themselves on the phone trying to figure who is coming and how many to prepare for. Respondez s'il vous plait. It is the civil thing to do. An invitation warrants a prompt answer. You generally do not have to call to say you will not attend unless the invitation says, 'Regrets Only'. To RSVP shows good manners, consideration, polish, and respect. Missing this little act of civility will make the host have to do extra work, whether on the front end or the back, and surely makes you suspect and probably the one the event organizers will talk about.

2. **WWWWHW- The Civility of Preparation**

   After you have RSVP'd and before you show-up jot down the answers to the following. I have included some hints for you as a starting point.

   - Who? - Who will be there, who invited you, who would be good to invite to join you, who have you made commitments to that may be there?

   - What? - What is the reason for the event or meeting, what should you bring to be prepared, what are the goals and objectives- yours, the invitee, your company, what time does it begin and end, what is success?

- When? - When will the event begin, when do you need to leave to get there on time?

- Where? -where is the event, where in the building, where can you park, and then of course what will you wear? Is it an event for bankers vs. music industry publicists?

- How? - how will you introduce yourself; how will you introduce the person you invited and to whom, how will you meet who you've come to network with, how will you follow-up, how will you report to your associates, your manager, people in your network?

- Why? - why are you going, why were you invited, why should they invite you back?

3. **First Impressions- The Civility of Showing up**

Now that you have arrived, according to Woody Allen that is 80% of the challenge...

You only have, according to Camille Lavington author of "You've Only got Three Seconds", three seconds to make a great first impression. Look at your watch right now and realize what three seconds is. Count it - one thousand, two thousand, three thousand—Shazam! You have been evaluated by everyone who saw you. They have already come to some conclusions about who you are, what you represent, your economic status, the level of your title, your type. You have been deemed approachable or not. You have been written in or written off.

What are the determining factors that make people draw conclusions within the first seconds of meeting? What we are all looking for is the civility of how you greet others. We make a mental note of whether we want to get to know you better if you are safe. We look for evidence that we have something in common that we operate by the same rules. Yes, these indicators are based on surface cues, but we use these impressions to make irreversible judgments.

What do you think the appraisals consist of?

- Image - grooming, attire, style …are you suitable to approach
- Power- presentation, body language, interaction with and from others …is their status higher… are they to be admired and cultivated as a valuable contact

- Civility- voice, tone, volume, consideration, etiquette, or lack thereof …are they to be tolerated or avoided

4. **Introductions - The civility of launching a relationship**

A vital part of networking is mastering the art of introductions—the refined skill of introducing yourself and the protocol of introducing others.

When introducing yourself be authentic and have creativity. Say your first and last name. It is best not to use your title i.e., Dr. or surnames i.e., Esq., or PhD. A self-introduction that is civil would include, a description of yourself, your business or company and something engaging enough to leave people wanting more. To be creative, have something interesting to say about why you are attending the event or who invited you or something relevant to the person the place or the occasion. For example: "Hello my name is Dennis Robertson. I am here with our CEO Deborah Wright. This is the first time our company Carver Federal Savings has sponsored the financial literacy workshop for the chamber. Are you a member?" This quick introduction gives all the pertinent information and creates an opportunity for more discussion that is relevant to both people.

It ends with an open-ended question that will ensure the person will be talking about their favorite topic, themselves.

When demonstrating civility when introducing others, the protocol is to introduce the least important person to the most important person. Acknowledge the most important person by looking at them, saying their name and letting them know you'd like to introduce them to the least import- ant person. "Mr. President, I'd like you to meet the newest addition to the white house staff, Jane Doe." To be civil you will include some background information on each person helping them find their common bond ensuring no awk- wardness. "Jane Doe grew up in Hawaii, and may I add, has a mean jump shot having played college basketball." There is power and civility in giving a wonderful introduction. The direction of the conversation and perhaps the relationship of the people you introduce depend largely on your skill. Make it a point to be a great introducer of people.

5. **Remembering names - the civility of really connecting**

Everyone's favorite sound is the sound of their name from someone who has expended the energy to remember them. People are so flattered when you remember their name. I attended a luncheon once with the current President of Xerox, Ursula Burns. We were briefly introduced and had a short conversation before she was whisked away to make her presentation. After she spoke, she was surrounded by so many clamoring to talk to her. She must have talked to at least 70 women that day after her presentation. When we ended up leaving the event at the same time as she got off the elevator she said, 'Good to meet you Cheryl Walker-Robertson'. Do you think she has a fan in me? Here's how to have Ursula Burns civility.

Be in the moment when you have a human moment with someone. Look them in the eye not at the door. Say their name at least three times during the conversation; associate the name with the person, their position; notice something special about them; connect them to their business card; ask them to spell their name for you; think about the name phonetically, and others you know by that name. There are not too many things more civil than to pay attention to people.

6. Conversation skills - the civility of small talk is really listening

Small talk is a very big deal. It is the best way to search for common ground. You move from topic to topic until you find the topic you both have an interest in.

Small talk allows you to learn about other people. It is also a way of finding mutual areas of interest. This takes great listening skills and that takes civility. The civility in this is caring, showing that you have the patience and the compassion to listen. Have you ever spent time with people in a networking situation and all they can talk about is themselves? It is the best conversationalist who spends more time listening than talking—a different twist on small talk. Listening may be the most civil gift you can give. "Look out for the interest of others. When listening be reminded to focus on them. Not to wonder how you look, what he thinks of you and what you should say next. Put them first by listening in rapt attention concentrating on the one in front of you forgetting yourself" (David Roper, Daily Bread).

"When we hold our tongues and listen, we communicate our care. For an open ear speaks volumes to a heart that's in despair" (Sper).

7. Nonverbal communication - the civility of body language

It is a scientific fact that people's gestures give away their true intentions. Have you ever seen someone smile with their mouth yet not their eyes? According to Albert Mehrabian, a pioneer researcher of body language in the 50's, the total impact of a message is about 7% verbal (words only), 38% vocal (tone, inflection, and other sounds), and 55% is nonverbal. Crossing your arms gives you the perception of being unapproachable. The ultimate civil nonverbal communication is the handshake. The civil handshake is a web-to-web interaction that includes a smile and eye contact. Please avoid giving the fishy handshake, the bone crusher and the preacher's handshake. Another important tip is to be conscientious of personal space. Remember it could be cultural as to how much space a person claims but generally, in a social setting, 4-12 feet is what is considered civil. The persuasive head nod. Slow nodding communicates that you are listening and interested. The fast nod demonstrates impatience and is not so civil. Mirroring is a great way to build rapport; that is moving and gesturing the same as the person you are talking to. I remember a networking session where four of us were chatting and a 5th person sort of stood in the wings wishing they were in the conversation. The groups' respective body language physically opened to include him, and he was grateful. I've seen groups reject someone who fair game tried to break into the conversation and the group would not allow it and rejected him—It was a hurtful gesture and certainly lacked civility.

8. **Business card protocol - the civility of the presentation**

There should be civility in the way we exchange business cards. A business card is a representation of you and your business. When you are no longer in the person's company, it is your business card that serves as a reminder of who you are, how you made them feel, and how best to follow up. It is with this understanding that we should consider the treatment and presentation of the business card. I remember being at a networking event and as the person was speaking to someone they had just gotten a card from the unconsciously started cleaning their nails with the card. Not very civil. I saw the person walk away with a look just short of shock. A few tips on business card presentation: always present a pristine business card that is without stains or dog ears. It's a good idea to have business cards cases in several places that you constantly replenish. When you are giving your card, present it with the writing facing the person receiving it. Dr. Ivan Misner, master networker and president of BNI says "the main reason for giving a business card is getting one". When receiving a card, spend a few seconds reviewing it helps to remember the person and offers an appreciation for its information and its quality. The next civil question is, now that you have this business card and the other 15 you've collected, what will you do with it? Will you mix it in the pocket with your business cards and those you've collected? If so, it may take a minute to pull out your next card to give someone without sifting thru all the cards you collected that evening. If there is a name tag holder another tip is to put all the cards in your name tag sleeve. Then you can hand the whole sleeve to your AA or have it ready for you to send out notes by knowing where you met whom. Another tip is to have go tiered strategy for follow up. You decide how to tier it and which tier gets which follow up. For example, Tier A could be a fantastic lead whom you promised information. You will place a follow-up call with the information the next day. Tier B could be someone interesting you'd like to spend more time with. You will send a note card inviting them out to lunch. Tier C could warrant a follow up email expressing your gratitude for meeting them. The suggestion here is to have a strategy that works for you and that demonstrates your networking civility.

9. **Networking strategies - the civility of givers gain**

At the end of the day, networking is a necessary activity for businesspeople and professionals and those that aspire to be and do better. You should have several strategies that change based on the circumstances. Is it better to go to networking sessions alone? (This way you can focus on all your new contacts and what you have to offer them instead of having to also focus on the person you brought to the event.) Is it better to have one other person to network with you who can give you great introduction and who you can introduce in a way that they cannot? Is it better to have a team with you giving you more access to work the room that you share business cards with after the event? What are the criteria for which strategy you choose?

10. **Social media - the civility of friending strangers**

Of course, this is a reference to friending and being friended on Facebook but have civility when networking with social media is a very contemporary issue. This is not something Letitia Baldridge ever had to consider in her first Executive etiquette book, Emily post either. These days we must all consider that you can't really erase from the internet. How important is it to have civility when n net? The question we should ask ourselves is would you say the words you type if you were in that person or persons presence? Yet another litmus test would be would you post that picture or pictures if your father or your great aunt monitored your site? Racial slurs, harsh criticisms, bullying and blatant abuse don't work in real life, and they really have no place in the social media networking either. Consider how your comments would be perceived before you actually post them. Mostly, think about maintaining a certain level of civility before you hit "post," because what you send will be a permanent reflection of your professionalism and your personality. These infractions to civility may never be erased and could be used against you. Employers and colleges are now searching social media sites to get another perspective of candidates. Despite its digital nature, social media networking is still about real relationships, real conversations, and as such, they should be treated with real decorum and real civility.

I invite you to test the hypothesis that an intentional approach to networking with civility will cultivate more meaningful relationships, both business and personal. Making civility a part of your DNA will not go unrewarded in fact acts of courtesy and compassion in our daily lives, while networking or not, will result in noticeable changes in our homes, our communities, our culture, our world. It will make others feel good about you being around and civility will make you feel good about being and doing the right thing. Networking with Civility—is the ultimate business tool. Please visit our Blog or send us an email or a video and share your success stories when using these tools. We would be delighted to hear from you.

❧ POWER TIPS ❧

- According to Inc. Magazine (2017), 99% of people who network are afraid of the follow-up. Power Move—follow-up. Follow-up places you in the top 1% of effective networkers. Powerful networks are in the follow-up.

- Invest time in making business friends. The process may be slow; however, the ROI is worth the investment.

- Oxford Economics (2012) reports that networking is the one of the best ways to find and keep meaningful business connections. Design your networking plan and get to work.

- When networking, think mutual benefits.

ℭ RENEE WEATHERSBY ℕ

Renee Weathersby is a consultant and founder of Robinson Etiquette Institute, an international consultancy specializing in business and social etiquette and International Protocol. She is an internationally certified etiquette expert with world-class training from some of the most prestigious etiquette schools in the United States and Europe and over 20 years of professional experience. She has additional training in United Nations Protocol and Global business management. Ms. Weathersby trains corporate executives, entrepreneurs, professionals, organizations, and college students, including adults and children, to help them successfully navigate any 21st-century business or social situation'.

Renee is a member of the Protocol - Diplomacy - Protocol Officers Association, Association of Talent Development, and the National Association of Urban Etiquette Association.

In her spare time, she loves to travel, read, and is a lover of all things Tea.

Robinson Etiquette Institute

4

THE HISTORY & ETIQUETTE OF AFTERNOON TEA

Renee Weathersby

There are few hours in life more
agreeable than the hour dedicated to
the ceremony know as afternoon tea.

Henry James

A brief history of tea Drinking

Promoting feelings of elegance and gentility, and served in every major city globally, there are few ceremonies considered more cultured than afternoon tea. Filled with rich traditions, there are various historical rules of etiquette to observe and social faux pas to avoid, from the proper way to stir your tea, to whether you should raise your pinkie. Exhibiting graceful dining manners is both a sign of respect and a way to showcase savoir-faire. The ceremony of taking tea has even adapted to the frenetic pace of the 21st century. Today's savvy businessperson knows that most business dealings are not conducted at the conference table or in the boardroom, but rather in social settings including tea rooms or an informal tea.

Historically, tea drinking has been around for over four thousand years and is considered a way of life for most countries. The discovery of tea is credited to Chinese Emperor Shen Nung in approximately 2737 B.C.E. Legend has it that while servants were boiling water, some leaves fell into the boiling water. Instead of removing the leaves, Shen Nung decided to taste the liquid, found it suitable for drinking, and called it té or cha. From Asia, tea was exported around the world.

Although tea is consumed worldwide, the British gave the world the ritual of afternoon tea. Tea arrived in England during the 17th century in London and was served in coffee houses to the aristocracy. Catherine of Braganza, the Portuguese wife of Charles II of England, is credited with introducing tea to England. She would hold grand tea affairs within her bedchambers for her female friends since women could not socialize outside the home. According to Jane Pettigrew, a world-renowned tea expert from the 1830s to 1840s, the afternoon tea party developed into a new social event that filled the gap between breakfast and dinner. In Europe, dinner time took place between the hours of 7:30 and 8:00pm. According to numerous historians, Anna Maria Russell, the seventh Duchess of Bedford and Lady in Waiting to Queen Victoria, is credited with the ritual of Afternoon Tea. Feeling faint during the long hours before dinner, Anna asked her servants to bring finger sandwiches and tea. Anna would invite other women over for finger sandwiches and tea, and a tradition was born. Queen Victoria, also a tea lover, promoted tea drinking by holding tea receptions in Buckingham Palace. By her reign's end, tea-drinking saturated the British aristocracy.

Tea was introduced to the Americas in the latter part of the 17th century by a Scotsman named Sir Thomas Lipton. Tea drinking was prevalent until excess taxation of Tea was imposed by Great Britain, which ultimately led to the Boston Tea party revolt in 1763.

America is credited with developing iced tea at the 1904 World's Fair in St. Louis, Missouri. Over the years, tea drinking waxed and waned in the United States, but afternoon tea today has made a comeback.

Finessing the Afternoon Tea

Invitations

Traditionally, invitations to afternoon tea were formal affairs and were mailed. If the venue was informal, invitations were extended through a phone call or face-to-face. However, in modern society, invitations can be extended through mail, telephone, text, email, or an electronic invitation website such as Evite, Punchbowl, or Greenvelope, depending on the formality of the tea event. The invitation provides the date, time, theme, place if there is a guest of honor, and any other instructions guests need to know. Invitations should be sent one to two weeks in advance.

Attire

Questions often come up about the appropriate attire for afternoon teas. Depending upon the venue, the proper attire for an Afternoon tea is primarily business casual or "smart casual," as the British would say. Sportswear, jeans, and tennis shoes are out. Some venues require more formal dress but always check with the host or venue for details about attire. Men do not need to wear a suit unless it is a business tea, but nice shirt, jacket, and trousers will do. Women could use this opportunity to dress up in a pretty dress or a nice pantsuit, hats, fascinators, and gloves. However, when wearing gloves to afternoon tea, they are removed upon entering the building. Keep it classy and fancy.

How to take tea

Here is a basic overview of the etiquette of taking afternoon tea. Afternoon tea is served from a sandwich plate or a three-tiered serving tray. The tea meal is divided into three distinct courses and eaten in the following order: savories (finger sandwiches), scones, and then pastries. The equipment on the tea table includes a teapot, creamer, and sugar), tea strainer, sugar tongs, a bone or porcelain China tea set (teacup, saucer, tea plate, or luncheon plate), a napkin, water glass, a dish for lemons, and flatware including a lemon fork. The napkin is placed folded on your lap after the host sits down.

First is the etiquette on how to hold a teacup. The teacup is held by pinching the handle between the thumb, index, and middle finger. Do not extend your pinkie finger while lifting the teacup. Extending the pinkie was the practice of the lower classes.

Secondly, if you're sitting at a table, the proper manner of drinking tea is by raising the teacup towards your mouth, with the spoon and the saucer on the table, then you place the teacup back on the saucer after taking the tea. It is considered rude to look elsewhere when you are drinking tea. You are to look into your teacup while sipping your tea. No slurping, please!

The saucer stays on the table: Please, do not lift your saucer with your teacup. Your saucer and your spoon are to remain on the table while drinking tea unless you are standing.

Do not blow on the tea if it is too hot, allow the tea to cool down before sipping the tea.

Stirring the tea should be done without clanging noises. The correct way to stir tea in the teacup is by moving the teaspoon back and forth the motion not touching the sides of the teacup.

It is okay to eat with your fingers: Do not be afraid or shy to put scones, sandwiches, or sweets in your mouth with your fingers. Do try a little of each course.

To eat scones, break them in half eating each half one at a time. Using a knife, spread the butter, jam, or clotted cream on the scone. Do not eat the scone like it is a sandwich.

Host and guest duties

Whether you are a host or just a guest at a tea party, there are certain duties that are expected of you, that will aid the success of the tea party:

Host duties

The host is responsible for handling every detail of the tea whether it is a tea party or the tearoom. The host selects the venue for tea, makes the reservation, and sends the tea invitation. The hotel, tea salon or tearoom should know that you are the host. As the host, you should arrive early and arrange for payment of the bill including the tip.

Normally guests are served tea from teapots if at a hotel, or tearoom by the wait staff. When at a tea party event or private home, the host serves the tea. At a large tea party, each table is assigned a host to serve the tea and the spout on the teapot will be turned towards the host. Before the end of the tea, the host discreetly leaves the table to take care of the bill if it has not been handled upon arrival. A savvy host will never allow the bill to be brought to the table.

Guest duties

When invited to tea, always RSVP (please respond) to the invitation. Do not ask or bring uninvited guests. If you cannot attend, please inform the host as soon as possible to cancel. The day before the event, reconfirm the place and time. Remember to dress appropriately according to the venue. Arrive on time and if you have not met the host, introduce yourself. If possible, go to the restroom before going to the table. Once you sit down you are expected to dine until the meal is over except in an emergency. Do not monopolize the host and make sure you mingle and chat with other guests including the guest of honor. Do not start eating until the host begins the tea and everyone has been served.

The host signals that the tea has ended by placing the slightly folded napkin to the right of the plate and will rise from their seat. Do not forget to thank the host/hostess before leaving.

When you reach your home, remember to send a thank you note to the host(s) for the invitation.

Finally, here are some things **not to do** at an afternoon tea:

- Place glasses, keys, cell phone or purse on the tea table
- Eat with your gloves on
- Dunk your scones in the tea
- Place the spoon on the saucer in the front of the cup
- Place a used napkin back on the table before the meal is over
- Talk with food in your mouth
- Overload your plate with food
- Remove or exchange place cards at the table
- Cradle the cup with your fingers or swirl the tea with your spoon

- Make slurping noises while drinking tea; tea is sipped

- Use cream in your tea because it will curdle

- Overfill the teacup if you are planning to add milk to the tea

- Squeeze lemons slices - instead, use the oil from the lemons to provide flavor

- Add milk to Darjeeling, green or white teas because it destroys the taste and texture of the tea

- Pour the tea, unless you are the host or wait staff

- Add milk and lemon to the tea because it will curdle.

Basically, relax and have a good time. Afternoon tea was meant for relaxation.

🌿 POWER TIPS 🌿

- When visiting a tearoom, know the etiquette before you go.

- Afternoon tea can be pricey and can cost anywhere from $15.00 to $360.00.

- The Afternoon Tea is a light meal, basically a snack so be prepared.

- Teatime is meant for relaxation. Enjoy teatime with yourself or with the company of others.

- Tea can be used in ways other than consumption.

- Explore the benefits of tea in facial steams, spa retreats, meditation mixers, and sleep.

- Explore the health and wellness benefits of tea. Did you know that tea aids in reducing eye swelling?

- Expand your taste buds with infused teas like lavender, peach, berries, and other flavors.

5

⁍DINING SKILLS

Renita Jackson

⌁

Good manners will open doors that the best education cannot

Clarence Thomas

Think no one is watching while you dine? Think again! Whether you're dining with a client, recruiter, prospective boss, current boss, associates, friends, or family, you should always follow the rules of proper dining etiquette because, someone is always watching.

Some people conduct business over a meal as a strategic way to get to know a person. Maybe you're on a date and you need to make a good impression. Or, maybe you're at an upscale event and you simply don't want to embarrass yourself. How you behave before, during, and after the meal tells a lot about your professionalism and social skills. Dining should be a pleasurable experience. Everyone and every age should practice good table etiquette. Knowing how to properly dine is a skill you will continue to use repeatedly.

Arriving at the table

You've been anxiously awaiting the arrival of this once in a lifetime gala event. Your attire is stunning, hair is immaculate, and you're wearing that special occasion perfume. When you enter the room, you know all eyes are on you. You graciously move through the banquet room. You sit down to a rather impressive dining table, meticulously set for a six-course meal that is fit for royalty. This exhilarating moment comes to a screeching halt as you look at the table and ponder "Which one of these glasses is mine? Why are there so many forks? What do I do?"

Maybe the event is not as formal, but just as important. The company's executive has invited you to join him for a business lunch at an upscale restaurant. You are being considered for a promotion with the company. The position requires you to dine with prospective clients. The company executive is testing your dining skills. This is an opportunity you don't want to blow. It could be that you're invited to dinner at the home of your fiancé's parents. You're meeting them for the first time. Your nerves are a tangled web, because you don't want to embarrass yourself by doing something uncivilized. Dining etiquette is the one area that puts most people in a manner's quandary, simply because of the fear of doing the wrong thing. Not to worry, this chapter will help you with the dining skills to navigate safely through any meal.

The place setting

Let's start with the basics. If there is a place card at the table with your name on it, it's there for a reason. That is where your host wants you to sit. This is not the time for you to play musical chairs by moving your name card to another location. Your host has painstakingly made the decision on the best seating arrangements for the event. Don't rearrange the place cards. If you don't particularly care for the person you are seated next to, you just have to suffer. Or maybe they are the ones who will suffer.

All place settings are arranged in the same order. The only difference is a formal place setting will have more pieces. The basic rule to remember about the table setting is the utensils are placed in the order in which they are to be used. When dining, you start with the utensils from the outside and work your way in. If you are still a little apprehensive about using the incorrect piece, follow the lead of your host or hostess.

Informal Place Setting

Formal Place Setting

Never forget what's yours

Sometimes table settings can be so close and tight that you don't' know what's yours and what's your neighbors. A quick way to remember is to form the smaller letters "b" and "d" with your fingers above your place setting. The b stands for bread and the d for drinks. Your bread plate is on the left side and your drinks or on the right side. All the other items that fall under and in between the bread plate and drinkware are yours too.

Napkin know how

Yes, there is napkin etiquette. The first rule is to make sure you use it, as many people will sit for a meal without using their napkin. When seated, place your napkin on your lap. If you are dining with a host/hostess, wait for them to place their napkin first. Large dinner napkins should remain folded in half, with the folded side to your waist. Smaller luncheon napkins can be opened all the way. Use your napkin to blot you lips and wipe your fingers if needed. Do not tuck the napkin into your shirt like a bib. Do not use your napkin to wipe perspiration from your forehead or to blow your nose.

Should you need to leave the table, but plan to return, place the napkin in the seat of your chair. This is a silent code to the server that you are returning to the table. Most fine dining restaurants will replace your napkin with a clean one before you return. Once you have completed your meal, lay your crumpled napkin on the table to the left side of the plate. Do not refold the napkin. Do not place the napkin in your plate. Do not stack your dishes or push your dishes away.

Utensils–what to do with them

There are basically two styles of dining, American and Continental. Each are acceptable. In American style dining you cut a bite sized piece of food with your knife and the fork with the tines down. Place your knife at the top of your plate in a resting position, turn your fork over tines up, lifting to your mouth and eat. In the Continental style, also cut your food with the tines down or push food onto your fork with the tines down. Lift the fork to your mouth tines down and eat while still holding the knife.

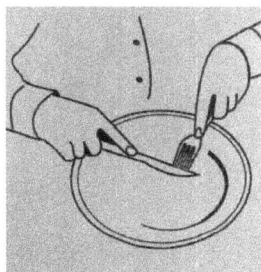

Holding Utensils

American style dining

Once you have used a utensil, never place it back onto the table. Just like the napkin, there is a silent code to be used with your utensils. There is a resting position for your utensils if you continue dining, and a finished position when you are done. Once you have finished dining, do not stack dishes, or push them away. The server has a method for clearing the table. If you are dining in someone's home, offer to help.

Eating soup

When eating soup, scoop the side of the spoon into the bowl and away from you. Carefully brush the bottom of the spoon off the side or back of the bowl, and then eat. This will help to avoid dripping soup on you. Scan the QR code to see a demonstration of the proper way to enjoy soup.

The Do's and Don'ts of dining

Besides the unspoken rules and silent codes, a lot of dining etiquette comes from things we learned while growing up. Here are some basic tips of dining manners as well as other tips that will keep you from embarrassing yourself or others while at the table.

- Don't place items such as keys, cellphones, wallets, or small cocktail bags on the table.

- Use good posture. Don't lean forward into your food. It's okay to lean slightly forward, but do not bend down into your food.

- Do not butter your entire roll or bread. Break a small bite sized piece, butter it and eat.

- Don't reach across the table for items. Politely ask someone to pass the item to you.

- If someone asks you to pass the salt or pepper, always pass both to keep the shakers together.

- Avoid adding salt, pepper, or any other condiments to foods before first tasting.

- Put small portions of food into your mouth and chew well.

- Don't chew with your mouth open.

- Don't talk with food in your mouth.

- Don't lick your fingers, utensils, or plate.

- No loud slurping or smacking noises with food or drinks.

- Don't blow on hot food to cool it down. Simply wait and enjoy some conversation.

- Don't dip your utensils into your water glass for cleaning. If your utensil is dirty, ask for another.

- Don't use your fingers or bread to push food onto your fork. Use your knife as the pusher.

- When dining family style, pass platters of food counterclockwise around the table.

- While at the buffet, always use utensils, not your hands, to place food onto your plate.

- Don't eat while standing at the buffet table.

What to do if?

If you get food stuck in your teeth, don't use a toothpick, your finger, or those terrible sucking noises to remove it. Try to discretely remove it with your tongue. If this is not successful, excuse yourself from the table to handle the matter.

If you drop your napkin or utensil on the floor, don't go under the table to retrieve it. Ask the server to bring you another one. If dining in someone's home, you need to pick up the item and inquire with the host/hostess on a replacement.

If someone drinks from your glass or picks up your utensil, don't address it. Discretely ask the server for another one.

If you need to remove something from your mouth such as an olive pit or bone, do so with cupped fingers over your mouth. Place the item on your plate, not under. You may use your napkin to cover your fingers while doing so, but do not spit the item into your napkin.

Many people say grace or pray before eating their food. It is okay for you to do so. If you do not and you are dining with someone and a blessing is said, simply remain quiet to show respect.

Ordering food and beverages

If dining with a potential client, a job interview, or a businessperson who is paying the bill, don't order the most expensive items on the menu. If you are not sure what to order, ask what they recommend. Don't order foods that are difficult to maneuver—like crab legs. Avoid ordering alcoholic beverages.

Making a Toast, don't burn it

Champagne toasts are generally done at celebratory events. If you are the "Toaster", don't bang on your glass with a knife to get everyone's attention. Simply ask, "May I have your attention please?" Those participating in the toast should avoid clanging glasses together. Agree to the toast by lifting your glass and saying "Cheers!" If you are the "Toastee", you do not drink to your own toast. After the toasting is complete, you can respond with a thank you and then drink.

RSVP

RSVP is French for Respondez s'il vous plait or Please Respond. This means the person who invited you wants you to accept or decline the invitation by notifying them. This is vital to the person planning the dinner or event. Respond in the manner requested—phone, email, or return card. Respond by the date requested or ASAP. Studies show only 30% of people RSVP.

Remember to compliment and thank your host or hostess for the meal. It's a nice gesture to offer to help with any clean-up if needed. If dining in a restaurant, remember to leave a tip.

Who pays for the meal?

This is something that should be considered before the bill arrives. If you simply asked friends or coworkers to get together for lunch or dinner, each person pays his or her own. If you have invited someone to lunch or dinner, you should pay. If someone asked to take you out, they will possibly pay, but may not feel obligated to do so; however, always be prepared to pay for your own without question or hesitation. It never hurts to ask to pay for your portion.

If you are paying the bill, you need to take care of the tip as well. Don't sit at the table with a calculator trying to figure out your portion of the bill and everyone else's. When ordering your meal, know how much your cost should be. Add tax, a generous tip, check the bill and be done. If you are paying for a business meal, you can arrange for payment in advance with the server or maître d' (the head waiter at a dining establishment). Discretely let them know you will handle the bill.

Whether dining with a client, a boss, friends, a job interview, or just at home, remember to put your best dining manners on display.

Enjoy your dining experience!

✾ POWER TIPS ✾

Tips to pull off good manners while dining:

- If in doubt, follow the lead of the host/hostess.
- Don't begin eating until everyone has been served.
- Utensils are placed in the order the meal is served. Use utensils from the outside and work your way inward.
- Eat at the same pace as the others at the table.
- When the host/hostess is done, so are you!
- Practice at home so you'll get it right in public.

Mastership of great culinary skills
enriches the wholeness
of a fine dining experience.

Wayne Chirisa

LAWANDA HOLLIMAN

Lawanda travels the world speaking and teaching on high performance in both leadership and company culture. As a retired Colonel of the US Army, she is a successful author, coach, speaker, facilitator, and a proven and trusted authority in high performance leadership and culture. She has trained leaders internationally from four continents. Lawanda founded Design High Performance in 2020 where she serves as the Lead Consultant. They help organizations reach top-tier execution and achieve their highest performance through innovative training, speaking, and leadership development. Prior to that, Lawanda completed nearly three decades leading teams spread across the Middle East and the US—where she developed the Supply Chain Management Blueprint, accounting for over $780 million in equipment. Lawanda has an MBA from Liberty University and a master's in strategic studies from the U.S. Army War College. She was commissioned at the University of South Carolina and earned an undergraduate degree from Columbia College with a major in mathematics. She has also served on several Boards over a twenty-year period. She spends her time now assisting organizations with how to design a workplace where High Performance is the Norm for leaders, teams, and the culture. Lawanda is a book junkie, she loves lighthouses, and enjoys great vegan food. She has two daughters, Elizabeth and Rebekah, and a family whom she absolutely loves and adores. She can be found traveling around the world meeting new people.

For more information about Lawanda, visit her website at www.designhighperformance.com, and her LinkedIn profile at https://www.Linkedin.com/in/Lawanda Holliman

6

CIVILITY IN LEADERSHIP

Key to a High-Performance Culture

Lawanda J. Holliman

ᴄᴄᵒᶻᵒ

Civility costs nothing
but buys everything.

Mary Motley Montagu

Having high performance leaders at the helm of an organization positions the company to address the declining social values negatively impacting the bottom line and company culture. Companies are trying to attract and retain top talent, engage employees, and create a thriving workplace that increases productivity and profits. Did you know that Employees' work effort, quality, and commitment to the organization are among the costs associated with incivility.

Furthermore, incivility can lead to a decrease in creativity and performance, a breakdown in team spirit, and negative customer responses. Managing such impolite behavior is costly.

High Performance Leaders address incivility in the workplace by intentionally introducing the concept of civility. They communicate the importance of civility. They address typical causes and effects of incivility and lessen the negative impact of incivility. In this chapter, you will explore skills needed to effectively practice civil behavior. The goal is to make high performance the norm for leaders, teams, and the culture.

The business landscape has shifted dramatically since the pandemic, social justice concerns and diverse generations working alongside eachother. People are becoming more impatient and ruder with each other, and companies will need to look at different ways that organizations systematize civility in the workplace. Companies concerned about retaining top talent and attracting more may need to rethink how they engage with their employees.

Imagine walking into the office and discovering an employee sitting at their desk with both hands pressed against their cheeks and a shocked expression on their face. The boss of the employee is yelling and pointing down at the computer and the employee. What three things come to mind when you consider that scenario? What are your thoughts? In a similar situation, what would you do? Consider your responses carefully. This is a 'fight or flight situation' if you are like many people. While the examples of the employee and boss may appear extreme, they represent uncivil behavior.

So, what is uncivil behavior in the workplace?

Workplace Incivility: Deviant workplace behavior of *low intensity* with ambiguous intent to harm the target that can include such behaviors as being rude, discourteous, impolite, or violating workplace norms of behavior.

While people may not always have malicious intent, uncivil behavior and its influence have a significant impact on team engagement, top talent retention, and company profitability. If some of the following examples match what you described:

- Rudeness and impolite behavior
- Disrespectful words or gestures
- Public reprimands
- Silent treatment

These actions described above are examples of uncivil workplace behavior. So, without delay, take a look (in no particular order) at five possible causes of uncivil behavior in the workplace. Consider the following reasons:

1. **Lack of Awareness.** The definition of uncivil behavior in the workplace statess that behaviors can be performed without the individual's full knowledge. Furthermore, there may be a lack of knowledge and awareness about the consequences of your actions. However, what you do and how you act can have a negative impact on team members and the organization. We'll talk about the cost of incivility later.

   You will come across cultural differences. You may have been raised with values, experiences, and ways of thinking that differ from those with whom you work. These distinctions are what distinguishes you and cause you to react differently than others in the same or similar situation. For example, your boss may come in and never greet employees; some may consider this rude, while others may see nothing wrong with it. They have different perspectives. For the time being, even if you are not always aware of when you are acting uncivilly, it is critical that you take steps to gain personal awareness of your actions and behaviors. A coach can assist you in overcoming this source of incivility.

2. **Anonymity.** Many people can get on digital platforms and say things online that they would never say in person in today's digital, interconnected world. Some people have found it simple to conceal their true identity in public. Nonetheless, they remain anonymous while making rude and impolite comments online. Training in online etiquette is required to help combat this behavior.

3. **Stress**. With all of the uncertainty, a global pandemic, and other health and well-being challenges, stress and uncivil behavior appear to be inextricably linked. Many people are filled with apprehension and fear about the future. How do you balance work, school, and finding time to relax and care for yourself? Taking care of your health is important for remaining civil. Some companies are also investing in wellness programs.

4. **Egocentric**. How many of you have experienced working with self-absorbed leaders or team members? According to dictionary.com, The term "egocentric" refers to thinking only of oneself, with no regard for the feelings or desires of others. If you work in an office where the leaders and your coworkers are only concerned with themselves, this can lead to uncivil and mean workplace behavior.

Make a note of where you are in relation to the following questions to perform a practical check on egocentrism. Who have you assisted in moving their careers forward? Have you ever had a conversation with someone who is very different from you? Who do you have scheduled for lunch? Now that you've answered these questions, in which of these areas do you need to get started helping others? What is your plan of action? Small steps can lead to big results in terms of team engagement, relationship building, and organizational culture strengthening. Being civil works.

5. **Legality versus Morality**. While some behaviors are not technically illegal, the habits formed as a result can certainly lead to the company's morale plummeting. Consider the company that failed to address the attitude of a top-producing leader who made demeaning comments to employees on a regular basis. While this attitude and habit were not technically illegal, they did undermine the organizational culture's moral values.

When you consider the moral fiber of the organization, you can create a thriving organization by ensuring that values are not only posted but acknowledged and adhered to in everyday performance. Examine your company values to see if any are out of sync with what it takes to make high performance the norm for your leaders, teams, and organizational culture. If incivility prevails, the benefits of assessing what values you want to follow as a company can pay off and save huge costs in more ways than one.

The cost of incivility

Why should your company be concerned about these uncivil actions? These behaviors come at a cost, and they have an impact on the overall culture of the organization.

The Cost of Incivility, written by Christine Porath and Christine Pearson, talk about a poll they conducted on 800 managers and employees in 17 industries to show how people's reactions play out. Among workers who have been subjected to incivility:

- 48% intentionally decreased their work effort.
- 38% intentionally decreased the quality of their work.
- 80% lost work time worrying about the incident.

Something that leaders must understand in relation to the statistics cited above from the Harvard Business Review article is that individual employees have an impact on overall performance and company culture. To begin, the physical and mental health issues caused by incivility will result in anxiety, depression, and increased stress levels in employees. Following that, performance suffers, resulting in poor work quality, high absenteeism, and subpar results. Finally, the company perception is one of high turnover, loss of corporate loyalty, and negative referrals. Leaders must make an effort to introduce civility in the workplace in order to attract and retain top talent, engage employees, and make high performance the norm for leaders, teams, and the culture.

> Culture is set from the top down,
> but it is implemented from
> the bottom up.
>
> Lawanda J. Holliman

What does workplace civility look like? Civility in the workplace will be characterized by employee engagement, customer loyalty, lower turnover, innovation and creativity, and a sustainable business in a high-performance culture. While we will not go into detail about these elements because they speak for themselves. Consider what it takes for leaders to begin introducing the concept of civility in the workplace.

What is the significance of culture? An organization's culture may be one of its strongest assets or its greatest liability, according to organizational psychologist. Indeed, it has been argued that organizations with a unique and difficult-to-copy culture have a competitive advantage (Barney, 1986).

Our next question is, "What is organizational culture?" Culture is defined as the organization's collective values, norms, and beliefs - also known as how things are done around here - and individual contributors play an important role in making those ideals about how things are done a reality. Looking at the day-to-day behaviors of individual leaders and teams is therefore important. That brings us to the topic of civility.

Civility is defined by Merriam Webster as civilized behavior, courtesy, politeness, or a polite act or expression. This is a good definition. However, there is another definition that addresses how civility can be used both individually and collectively within organizational culture. Civility is defined by the Institute of Government as "claiming and caring for one's own identity, needs, and beliefs without degrading someone else's." This definition assists leaders and your company in better understanding that anything sustainable is done by people—leaders and team members are the individuals who bring the organization's values, ideas, and identity to life.

Reality Check!

Let's be honest: Culture is established by leaders, but it also requires individual contributions to be carried out—and being civil at all times is not easy. Maybe you can recall a time when you didn't want to be civil in certain situations. You might not be considering it right now (smiling face). Anyone who can think of any uncivil act that tries to show up in their behavior, on the other hand, would want help overcoming it, right?

Maybe all you needed was a framework in your toolbox to help you and your teams better understand how to implement workplace civility. You only need to look to the following section of this chapter for strategies to assist you in achieving your goal of creating a civil culture in which leaders and teams thrive.

Civility is the link that connects poor interactions with others to better, more meaningful interactions that foster a high-performing culture. Leaders should demonstrate civility in all interactions.

How do you lead with civility? Set the example.

As the leader, you must set the example. Take steps toward greater civility by using this easy to remember S.T.A.R.T. framework.

Step 1: Start with Awareness

Leaders set the tone. The company environment and atmosphere is set by leaders. Therefore, as a leader, be conscious of your actions and how they appear to others. According to the Harvard Business Review, 25% of managers admitted to bad behavior and being uncivil because their leaders were rude. Make a point of introducing and modeling civil behavior on a consistent basis.

Step 2: Talk to Others.

Leaders go first. Leaders will initiate communication with team members. When you initiate conversations there is an increase in your opportunity to learn and value the diversity of thought. When you can bring your authentic self to someone else and allow them to do the same, you learn better ways to communicate. The keys to talking with others are honesty and authenticity. Genuine conversation can foster trust. Civility, respect, and humility should be used to frame the conversation.

Step 3: Active Listening.

Leaders listen with purpose. Listening is a skill that leaders must master in order to perform at their best. Prior to needing to be understood, seek to understand. Listening is an often-overlooked leadership tool that has the power to alter the outcome of any interaction. Learning to actively listen will help you frame better questions. Better questions can lead to innovative and creative solutions to business problems.

Step 4: **R**espect Differences.

Leaders Value Difference. Leaders with high emotional intelligence can control and express their emotions while handling interpersonal relationships judiciously and empathetically when disagreements arise. Another tool your company can use is the emotionally intelligent communication training. The outcomes are immediately apparent.

Step 5: **T**hink Strategically

Leaders consider options purposefully. Leaders must be able to recognize the relationships, complexities, and implications of a situation; anticipate possible outcomes; and plan what to do. Every leader should be aware of when the environment becomes uncivil in order to seize opportunities to implement a civil standard. The benefits of putting a plan in place to thrive are enormous.

When incivility comes your way, you can be a thermometer and react, or you can be a thermostat and set the temperature.

Lawanda J. Holliman

Why should Leaders be civil, introduce and promote workplace civility?

Leaders, in terms of the company environment and workforce populations, in the twenty-first century are concerned with attracting and retaining top talent as well as optimizing performance. This is an era of new beginnings. In the midst of a new normal, innovative ideas about how and where work is done, as well as how team members interact with each has evolved. An example is found in how standard work hours have shifted from a traditional 9-5 schedule to an around-the-clock connection for global engagement. Given that an organization's most valuable competitive advantage is its people, what work style should the culture encourage? The one in which high-performance is the norm.

Civility changes culture.
Add value in everything you do,
everywhere you go, and to
everyone you meet.

Lawanda J. Holliman

⚘ POWER TIPS ⚘

- Start with awareness. Being aware of one-self and others aids in the development of interpersonal skills necessary for workplace growth and productivity. Leaders can use the emotionally intelligent communications training course tool in conjunction with coaching to gain greater awareness. Leaders develop these skills while remaining authentically true to themselves.

- Another reason to practice civility. Leaders need positive outcomes and results. Leaders who develop a strategy thrive. Modeling civility enables leaders to capitalize on the talents and resources that contribute to long-term success while also allowing employees to thrive in the company culture.

- Remember, people are the competitive advantage. Every leader requires interpersonal relationships. To thrive, the company culture must allow individuals and teams to take an active role in shaping the culture as a valuable member of the team.

- Make high performance your norm. Consider hiring a coach. Working with a coach with proven experience can mean the difference between theory and reality. A coach can provide a safe space for leadership effectiveness and organizational performance development.

7

THE ETIQUETTE ADVANTAGE: EARLY BEGINNINGS

Trudy Snaith

The hardest job kids face today
is learning good manners
without seeing any.

Fred Astaire

Overall, a civil society benefits from the courteous behavior of its individuals and by extension, their use of good manners and etiquette. For success in life, or accomplishing the goals you wish to achieve, is accomplished by understanding and using the internationally proven guidelines of interacting with others. Fortunately, this expert advice is easy to find through self-education or programs offered by certified etiquette and protocol professionals.

Just imagine how different it would be if etiquette was a practiced way of life that came easy or naturally—something you really did not have to think about. You could then concentrate on building relationships or the business at hand. That is the impetus behind starting etiquette education at an early age. By the end of this chapter, you will:

- Understand the importance of early etiquette education.

- Be able to tailor a few etiquette basics for adults, to a child's level.

- Know what basic key areas children should be able to master

- Have simple exercises to help the youngest children learn and remember new etiquette skills.

Starting early—when and why

The simple answer is—the earlier one starts anything, the more time there will be to perfect that skill to the point that it develops into a natural way of life. Repetition is the key, repetition builds memory.

Parents often ask me how soon they can start teaching etiquette to their children. The answer is— right from the beginning. Children are like sponges; they imitate adults and absorb everything.

The youngest group I have taught etiquette to were three-year-old nursery school students. The program was very successful. The children absorbed everything presented to them and demonstrated the skills perfectly when asked. So, it is never too early. I am certain, though I have yet to try, children younger than that age are just as receptive. It is a matter of presenting the information in a way that will get the message across.

More important than delivering etiquette rules and basics is helping individuals understand that a lifestyle based on principles of etiquette will improve the quality of their life.

Areas to address

I have chosen to focus on a few key etiquette basics regularly covered in etiquette and protocol workshops for adults. I will tailor them to a child's level and the benefits of learning the skills early can be expected in many different interactions.

For successful social and professional interactions, adults must have a basic knowledge of internationally accepted etiquette and protocol rules of the following:

- The importance of self-presentation
- Introductions
- Adequate conversational skills
- Dining skills

Laying the groundwork for these skills early in life gives children and young adults an advantage that automatically puts them ahead of others.

The importance of presentation

It is human nature to form an opinion of a person the moment you see them. Before you even open your mouth to dazzle them with whatever you have to say. When I mention this in workshops and classes, the response I get is "But it's wrong and you are not supposed to judge people on the way they look." That may be true, but the reality is different. People will silently make their assessments and base their opinions on that assessment.

Back to how one can go about teaching the important concept of first impressions to children. Children like the feeling of having control over what they are going to wear. Some of their choices are enough to make you cringe but not wanting to dampen their spirits, parents usually give in. The teaching opportunity here is to gently reinforce the fact that what is worn by the child should be clean and not in need of repair. The adult should comment appropriately "You look very nice in that shirt", "That dress will make a good impression on Aunt Sue", "That's your favorite pair of shorts, isn't it? Why don't you put them in the laundry so I can wash that spot out?" If you do not have success with that—do not belabor the point. There will be many other opportunities. Treated as a normal occurrence, the idea is to plant in the child's mind that people pay attention to what they see, and thought should be given to how they present themselves to others. It will eventually sink in. Going one step further, simple personal hygiene should also be addressed. A child should not be allowed to greet guests or approach the dining table with mud all over their face. Yes, I know that is an extreme example, but you get the idea.

Introductions

The etiquette basics of introductions for adults involve things like direct eye contact, a good handshake, an awareness of precedence, and good conversational skills. These can all be mastered by children at appropriate age levels.

Eye contact. A person who avoids eye contact is viewed suspiciously so we do not want that habit to even start. Children as young as three years old can be encouraged to look directly at someone when speaking to them. The best method at the youngest age is gentle reminders. Older children often need to be reminded of direct eye contact as well. For all ages this is very important to establish.

Handshakes. It is possible to teach five-years-old children and maybe younger, a proper handshake—but only as an introduction. The size of their hands limits overall success in this task. It is only when they are about seven years old and older that their hands are a manageable size for executing a proper handshake easily. In these Covid-19 times of social distancing, shaking hands has been discouraged. But the feeling is that eventually, it will return as an accepted way of greeting. Therefore, learning the rudiments of a good handshake is good preparation.

Precedence. Business etiquette courses go into detail about how to prepare for professional encounters where knowledge of addressing individuals based on their 'importance' is crucial. Clients or dignitaries place a lot of importance on this recognition. If you get it wrong, they will not correct you, but it will affect their decision making. Learning the mechanics of this at any age is advantageous. Having this knowledge early takes the pressure off it being a distraction to 'get it right' at important moments in the young person's future. So, making it a part of early etiquette education puts one ahead of the crowd.

Learning the rules of introductions is a tricky one and a totally new concept for children. The idea of this exercise is to establish in the young person's mind the etiquette rule dictating that thought must be given when addressing people. This will be especially important in their futures when knowledge of correct protocol could make or break a business deal. It also indicates to the person the adult is dealing with (who may be very important!) that the person they are interacting with knows what they are doing. What we want to do here is train the child's mind now, to give them plenty of time to practice this skill and so it becomes second nature to them.

When introducing one person to another, precedence dictates that you must recognize the importance or 'standing' of the people involved and address them accordingly. It sounds confusing but is quite simple. We divide people into specific groups:

- Children
- Teens
- Adults
- Senior citizens
- Very Important people (VIP's)

Of those groups, we further consider their age and note if they are male or female. I do want to sidestep a moment here to mention that gender diversity has added another layer of consideration to this process. Therefore, the person making this introduction based on precedence must, to the best of their knowledge, factor in current gender diversity principles.

You get started by saying the name of the person of the most 'importance' first. Learning this fact is the ultimate etiquette instruction for introductions. I have found it best to teach young people to take their time and think about what they are going to say before they open their mouths. There is no rush. You want to introduce two people and keep it simple. "I would like you to meet" is the simplest thing to say and all that is required. No need to get fancy with "Let me introduce, May I present" or all those other things we hear on television.

'(most important person)', I would like you to meet '(person of next importance down)'.

Based on another set of the group:

'(a senior citizen)', I would like you to meet '(a teen).

For two people in the same group, you factor in age and gender. Gender first then age. And VIP's trump all.

Young people should always call adults by their last name unless given permission to do otherwise. When introduced to someone the proper response is "It's nice to meet you."

Having to stop and think about what you are going to say before you say it, makes better conversationalists. There are lots of other precedence rules but this basic one is an important one to lay the groundwork of for young people. Once learned, it will serve them royally.

Dining skills

This I believe, is the favorite of most people seeking etiquette advice. I know it is the favorite of all boys in my etiquette classes, probably because I feed them! It is enjoyed because people have an opportunity to showcase the skills they have learned and become so proud of mastering.

For young people, the etiquette goals of dining skills are:

* Learning the placement of what to touch on the table. The plate in front of them, fork to the left of the plate, knife to the right of the plate, water glass above the knife and bread plate above the fork.

* The difference between continental style dining (the knife and fork are always picked up, used, and replaced at the same time) and American style (cutlery is picked up together, used to cut what one is going to eat then the knife is placed across the top of the plate to 'rest' until required again) can be confusing. For continental style, the fork tines remain pointing down during use. For American style, the fork begins tines pointing down and after the knife is placed at the top of the plate, the fork is used tines facing up. That is why it is often referred to as 'zig-zag' style of eating.

- Where to place the cutlery when resting during the meal and where to place it to indicate one is finished. (Illustrations in sample section). This is called 'silent service'. Learning this is interesting and fun for young people. It is useful in helping the wait staff recognize where the diner is during their meal. The diner can then focus on conversation with others in their group without the interruption of being disturbed by wait staff.

- One challenge for young people here is learning to hold the cutlery correctly in their hands. Personal hands-on instruction and practice is required.

- Diners should know that items like bread, butter, etcetera are passed to the right at the start of the meal and then whatever is logical thereafter.

- Learn what to do with foods they do not like. Unless they are allergic, I urge young people to at least try the food item. If they have allergies, they should tell the hostess in advance.

- Learn to use the napkin correctly to catch crumbs on their lap and wipe their mouths during the meal, especially before taking sip of their water or beverage.

- Be encouraged to make polite conversation throughout the meal.

- Stay at the table until everyone is finished eating. If they must leave, they should ask the hostess if they may be excused. Young people should not get in the habit of getting up and down from the table during a meal.

- And always show appreciation to the hostess at the end of the meal.

The Executive School of Protocol website is being updated and under construction. Please feel free to contact me by email: tsnaith@gmail.com with questions about the etiquette skills mentioned in this chapter.

Cutlery Positions

Continental resting position   American resting position

American finished position

American finished position

Continental finished position

POWER TIPS

- Repetition is important when teaching young people etiquette basics. It builds memory."

- Setting an example goes a longer way than words.

- Mealtimes are excellent opportunities to practice conversational skills and allow young people to express themselves. Young people enjoy being included.

- Though there may be only one or two young people in the family being introduced to etiquette education, it is best shared by reviewing with the child what they have learned.

- Gentle reminders by using the correct format yourself, not embarrassing the young person in front of people, work best when corrections are necessary.

8

TEN RULES OF ENGAGEMENT FOR EVERYDAY LIFE ETIQUETTE

Cheryl Walker-Robertson

Rule #1:

Improve your business etiquette.

Did you know that facial expressions are the only non-verbal communication that are universal? Do you always think that your message starts the moment you speak? Perhaps this is a good time for a Protocol International session for your company.

Watch your Protocol Ambassador, Cheryl Walker-Robertson, as she talks about *7 General Tips to Improve Business Etiquette Fast*

Rule #2:

Make the best of videoconferencing.

Currently, Zoom videoconferencing is the go-to tool for video calling. Choosing a virtual background for any call has become a staple for many businesses. However, please be conscientious when using a background. It is part of your presentation.

Four Protocol Tips to Virtual Background

1. Use it to mask your surroundings. Virtual backgrounds offer an alternative to masking a messy room.

2. Set the right tone. The right virtual background can set the tone, feel, or vibe of a meeting. It is a business meeting or social gathering?

3. Conversation point. A virtual background can be a great conversation topic or starter for a session. Use it to emphasize a point or to get a message across – get creative.

4. Showcase your personality. Virtual backgrounds can also be used to express oneself in communicating personality and feelings. What image best reflects you?

Rule #3:

Speak with confidence when making a Toast to acknowledge special occasions and people.

Celebrations are something we look forward to throughout life. Be sure to mind your manners when attended various holiday events. Your protocol team is here to give you our Top Ten Protocol International Tips for Toasting.

1. Allow the host to lead.
2. Remember timing is everything.

3. Don't grab a knife and bang on the stemware for attention.

4. Wondering when to stand? 7 or less remain seated, 8 or more stand to make the toast.

5. You don't need alcohol in your glass to toast.

6. Protocol would say don't clink the glasses just raise them. Etiquette suggests if someone approaches your glass to clink, give in and do it. Perhaps they don't know the protocol.

7. A Toast is not a roast. Keep it short and sweet.

8. Don't run around the room clinking every glass. A raised glass has more class.

9. Don't forget to toast the host.

10. Speak confidently and project your voice according to ambient noise.

Rule #4:

Flex your etiquette muscles when working out.

Okay, so you're a gym rat, you're consistent in your attendance and focused on your goals to achieve the best fitness results possible. You know your way around the gym, you don't skip the warm-up and you understand the importance of proper technique in weightlifting to prevent injury. You enjoy the experience, look forward to going and always feel better, healthier when you leave.

But wait, what about those annoying, disrespectful gym goers that sometimes make the experience less than enjoyable. You know who we mean, the ones that miss the importance of good etiquette while working out by treating the gym, the equipment and other gym goers improperly. That's not you, is it? If it is, the injury you might sustain could be to your reputation.

Whether you're new to the gym or a total gym rat, it's always good to keep up with proper gym etiquette. So, we are here to save your reputation by offering a few tips that keep everyone's gym experience enjoyable and productive.

1. Wear the proper attire.

   The gym is for one purpose and that's working out not to distract others. Wear proper gear based on your workout.

2. Consider your personal hygiene.

   The amount of sweat you produce at the gym may indicate that you're working hard, but it only looks good if you smell good. There is nothing wrong with working up a sweat, but if you give off an odor that affects the entire atmosphere of the gym it can be pretty distracting, to say the least.

3. Maintain an awareness of your surroundings.

Exercising comes in all forms so be cognizant of personal space. Others may require more room, so make sure to give yourself enough space to work out while giving others enough space as well.

4. Be courteous and considerate.

We all have our favorite machine, but it may also be someone else's favorite. Keep your work out to a minimum and respect any time limits posted per machine. Before taking over any equipment, ask those who are near the equipment, if it is being occupied.

5. Manage the use of equipment.

Rack your own weights and spray the down the equipment after you use it. Be mindful when asking someone to spot you. Most people in workout mode are really focused.

6. Protect your belongings.

   Make sure to keep your belongings out of the space of others or get a locker for your personal things – most gyms will provide lockers or space to store your items.

7. Keep the peace.

Finally, avoid the drama that distracts others. Eliminate the noise, make sure your headphones and conversations with others are at a normal volume; and avoid dropping weights or equipment on the ground.

Rule #5:

Slow your roll in the drive-thru.

Yes, there is etiquette to follow at the drive-thru

We all want to get out of the drive-thru quickly to continue with our chores. To make this day-to-day experience smoother for us, the employees, and all the cars in line, it all starts with remembering that a drive-thru is for small orders.

1. A drive-thru is made for small orders with expediency in mind.

2. Avoid tailgating the car in front of you – leave space in case of an emergency.

3. Know the order you want to place before arriving at the speaker and speak clearly.

4. Arrange payment method before arriving at the window to pay.

5. Once at the pay window or window to collect your items, no add-ons please.

6. If a mistake is made with your order, park and go inside to rectify.

Rule #6:

Know the Do's and Don'ts of workplace cell phone use.

I was once invited to participate in a business meeting that was held in DC. It was with a group from the company's HR department discussing protocol and etiquette training as a part of their onboarding. As I was escorted to the board-room eleven minutes before the start of the meeting, another person was also entering the room on their phone. The assistant tried introducing me but could not succeed because they well were occupied by their phone. A second person entered the room on a call seemingly ordering refreshments for the meeting, gestured hello, and then walked out of the room again. Lastly, a third individual came in, greeted me, introduced themselves, sat, and then made a call.

Once the executive arrived for the meeting everyone immediately hung up (yet the phones rang and buzzed throughout the entire meeting). Let's just say, I hope they will join the new employees for the Protocol International training one of the topics the committee decided on was Techno Etiquette!

If you see the same scenes playing out within your organization and it is one of your pet peeves, consider bringing Protocol International's program on Techno Etiquette to your organization. In the meantime, here are a few tips on the next pages for cell phone use in the workplace.

Protocol Tips for Cellphone Usage in the Workplace

1. When entering the workplace, make sure ringer is off.

   Nothing is worse than having your favorite song on your ringtone blasting through the office when your cell phone rings. If your ringtone is a simple default ringtone that comes with your phone, it is still best to make sure your phone is on silent.

2. Avoid accessing and answering your cell phone while engaged in conversation.

While engaged in conversation with a colleague, give them your undivided attention. It is very rude to interrupt a face-to-face conversation to pull out your cell phone to answer a call or text while someone is speaking to you. Avoid the urge to do this, it will be appreciated.

3. Take personal calls in private.

Taking personal calls in a professional environment isn't exhibiting respect for the workplace. Your colleagues may not be interested in hearing your personal conversations. It is proper protocol and etiquette to retreat to a private area to take these calls.

4. Do not use your phone during meetings.

Using your phone during meetings is disrespectful and gives the impression that something more important has your interest. It is important to give your undivided attention to the speaker or the topic being discussed as a matter of respect and so that you don't miss important information pertaining to your job. Please do not have your phone out or even periodically check it under the table during a meeting. Unless it is absolutely necessary for you to be reached, leave your phone at your desk during meetings.

5. Do not have cell phones out at business lunches/ dinners.

Cell phones are not a part of the place setting at the dining table. Please keep them in your purse or pocket during your business breakfast, lunch, dinner, or tea. (Note Tip's #2 & #4)

Rule #7:

Introduce yourself to be rememebered.

Did you know that 60% - 80% of all job connections are made through networking? Professional networking is very important for creating lasting impressions. Knowing how to effectively introduce yourself to a potential employer, client, or business partner is a crucial part of successful networking.

Seven Tips for Executing a Powerful Introduction:

1. Wear a friendly face and smile.

2. Say your first and last name.

3. Tell an interesting fact about yourself.

4. Explain what you do (not just your job title).

5. Be short and to the point.

6. End with an open question to receive a follow-up response.

7. Understand when it's your turn to listen and respond back.

Politeness and an affable address
are our best introductions.

Marcus Tullius Cicero

Rule #8:

Show up for special events in a special way.

What a moment in history, the inauguration of the 46th President Joseph R. Biden, Jr., and Vice President Kamala Harris, the first woman, first Black, and first south Asian vice president of the United States of America. The peaceful transfer of presidential power from one administration to the next is a hallmark of American democracy. Like many other historic and traditional ceremonies that occur internationally, protocol is critical for such ceremonies for the sake of pomp and circumstance and order. Everybody understands the rules, what's appropriate, where to sit, when to stand, etc. It's always best to know what to expect, what your role is, and how to be. Please consider these standard protocol tips for how you too can show-up.

1. Rock your Grand Entrance

2. Cross the aisle to speak before the program starts.

3. Do your research, be considerate and brilliant when you plan your attire. *[Suffragette white? Democrat Blue or unity Purple? Pants or skirt? College baseball cap, Fedora, or nothing?]*

4. Know the protocol for the ceremonies; review the itinerary and if you can, the guest list.

5. Know the players involved. Not just the leaders and celebrities but who should you know in the background the team responsible for the success of the event.

Rule #9:

Use etiquette when texting.

Do you ever find yourself challenged when texting and receiving texts? Like...How soon should you text people back? How many emojis are too many? Do you use exclamation points, commas, apostrophes, and periods?

Let's discuss texting behavior in this Protocol International episode. It's become quite an art form over the past decade or so. Though widely accepted, there are protocol and etiquette rules yet mostly unspoken, and unwritten. The thing is people probably won't tell you, but you could be accidentally sending mixed signals that could affect your brand.

Luckily, you have a protocol ambassador that addresses these issues and I have some tips for you to ensure we are all better at texting.

1. Use emojis judiciously

   Everyone uses emojis these days. In a text-based form of communication with no indication of tone or intent, emojis add meaning and nuance to your texts. Sometimes we run the risk of coming off bland. or sometimes our texts can get lost in translation. This week Sprinkle them into some of your messages but please consider the context. As in, maybe don't use the kiss emoji for your boss. But if you're texting a friend, an associate, a prospect- a smiley face could go a long way.

2. Watch your punctuation

   Punctuation is big a deal. But texts are not the same as email or formal letters. sometimes You're better off not using punctuation.   to sound neutral. to change the tone.

   Quantity matters, too. A single exclamation point is fine for a coworker or a casual acquaintance. But if you're talking to your bestie, feel free use liberally. Without exclamation points in a casual, friendly text, you might as well be using a period!!

3. Don't send a million texts

    The worst thing Is getting 16 texts back-to-back, In the span of 30 seconds. Have you ever been on a zoom or in a meeting with that person getting back-to-back texts? Wow!

    Maybe at some point you might want to just pick up the phone and call.

4. Don't use all caps

    Unless it's mutual, like when you and your brothers are yelling at the EAGLES. otherwise. no screaming.

5. Use the right laughter level

Are you LOLing? ROFL? What about an LMAO? A great way to indicate lightheartedness even sarcasm but be careful which you use for whom.

Rule #10:

Make a great first impression.

We can't talk about the art and science of networking without talking about the critical issue of First Impressions.

In the science of a first impression is the event when one person first encounters another person and forms a mental impression of that person.

The first impressions individuals give to each other could greatly influence how they are treated and viewed. In business it can mean the difference in getting the position, the promotion, the deal or most important - the trusted relationship.

First Impressions will always be the barometer people use to determine status, authority, trustworthiness, competence, likability, confidence, or lack thereof.

These judgements are made at lightning speed. They are based on instinctive responses in the brain's emotion processing center, the amygdala.

Some people conclude a stranger is reliable because he or she looks like someone trustworthy, or they make judgments based on stereotypes.

Thing is, you can control these visual cues.

It's what people use to judge us and guess what, its' also how we judge others. Honestly, impression accuracy varies depending on the observer and the person being observed. We at Protocol International humbly submit that this is an opportunity for all of us to manage the compelling concept of perception. It is very hard to use the second impression to change the first. We never get a second chance to make a first impression.

Be the best guest when visiting someone's home.

INTERVIEW WITH THE EXPERTS

An interview with Trudy Snaith

What sparked your interest in teaching etiquette to young children?

When I first moved to Bermuda, I worked in the health department with the prenatal unit. In teaching prenatal classes with parents, I had a captive audience. The thing I noticed most about children who were going into primary kindergarten and grade one, was their inability, seemingly, to sit still and listen. You miss a lot by not listening. And, though young children are in an exploration stage of learning, if they are not actively taught how to actively listen, poor communication skills are reinforced. Seeing what I saw with the children, I was motivated to work with young people.

What is the risk, or the disadvantage for children who do not learn some of the basic etiquette skills you discuss in your chapter?

The risk is not learning or understanding basic interpersonal skills that potentially impact both personal and professional worlds. I'm thinking of a specific time when a social worker asked me to work with a group of young girls on social etiquette. Usually when I worked with a small group, the children would be seated in a small area, waiting for the teacher to appear. However, in this case, the girls, who ranged from 10 – 13 years of age, were roaming about the room and shouting across at one another. They were interrupting one another and using inappropriate language. After calming the scene and meeting the girls on day one of my assignment, I went home and rethought my lesson plans. It was obvious that what I had in mind, initially, was not going to work with this group. By the end of the course the girls had learned several important lessons about how to interact more appropriately, especially when they had an important message to share with others. For me, it is not okay to allow young people to remain the way they are, if their behaviors are not productive or conducive to their betterment. Young people understand and expect boundaries. That will not stop them from constantly testing them, but it is the responsibility of teachers to set those boundaries and not be tempted to lower the bar. This is a principle of mine that I do not waiver from. Poor etiquette is equal to ineffective communication. That creates a disadvantage.

So, that kind of shifts perspective a bit. It seems as if a curriculum of this sort would be appropriate in schools.

When you're talking about conversational skills, dining skills, and standards of how we behave or interact in society, yes, they can be integrated within the public education system. Those are basic skills for success and should be addressed in the school system at some point. Sure, this would suggest a change in the existing curriculum, but it is a worthwhile adjustment and can be done in collaboration with etiquette experts. The syllabus I designed to work with young children is very flexible. When I go into a classroom the first day of working with children, I first make an assessment, then tailor my syllabus to the culture of the class. The principles are basic enough to allow for this variety. It comes down to presentation and making sure students understand and can apply them. When you show them how the skills translate into everyday life skills, they become more meaningful. I explain the importance of each skill I teach and make learning fun.

Talk to me more about Introductions. This was a particularly interesting topic because I did not realize the etiquette details, but they make sense.

The topic of Introductions is so important because this is where people make a first assessment of who you are. When I teach this to children, I want to do the basics. I want them to be able to apply the skills immediately when they practice with their parents and other relatives. Like other skills, they learn the etiquette of introductions through repetition. When making an introduction, we must remember that this is not a process to be rushed because once you say what you say, you can't take it back. What you say, how you say it, and body language influence how you are viewed when meeting someone for the first time. There really is an art to the interchange that takes place in introductions.

What's one suggestion or recommendation do you have for teaching young children dining skills?

Simply put, a meal is not just about you and the food you consume. A dining experience is about you and the people around you. I can recall some horrifying ordeals with parents and children in restaurants. In the restaurant is not the place to teach etiquette. You can reenforce skills in the restaurant, but you want to teach skills in the home. I can't count the number of times I have seen this mistake. You must keep in mind that what's happening at your table may be an interruption to everything that's happening at another table. In most cases people go out to dinner to enjoy a meal and the company they are with. You must be aware of the impact of what's happening at your table on everyone else. Dining experiences can be overwhelming for small children. There is a lot of external stimulation, and it may be difficult for little ones to adjust to this environment. In this case, awareness of the type of restaurant you select is important.

An interview with Renita Jackson

Your chapter, you are detailed in your explanation of how to do a proper introduction. Why is this topic so important?

First, it is important to simply acknowledge people when you are in their presence. On my morning walk along a trail this morning, I was reminded of this gesture. As I moved along the trail, an older gentleman approached going in the opposite direction. Right as he was in proximity, he looked me in the eyes, tipped his hat, and continued about his way. I thought to myself, "It sure is nice to meet who remind you that there is kindness and common courtesy in the world." The topic of introductions is important because it is a way of acknowledging others, a way of simply saying, "I see you."

Where did you get your start in the interest of etiquette?

For me, etiquette is a lifestyle. I grew up learning about etiquette in my household as a young child. My mother is a Southerner from Alabama and taught us many lessons early on. She loved to host and entertain others in our home. As early as I can remember, we seemed to have company of some sort in our home. My mother wanted everything she did to be nice, neat, and orderly. She had the Amy Vanderbilt book of etiquette and referred to it for many different occasions. If she, my sister, or I had a question about how to do something, if she thought it was addressed the book of etiquette, we would have to remove the book from the shelf and read up on the topic. Though you don't hear much about charm school nowadays, then it was such a thing and my older sister attended school at the local Sears and Roebuck. I was too young to go with my sister, but I remember being so excited about the binder my sister received and carried back and forth with her to charm school. By the time I was old enough to attend charm school, the course was no longer offered. It was years later, but I did get formal training to become a Certified Etiquette Consultant. This is truly a passion of mine.

What would you say to the college grad or corporate person about the importance of etiquette?

I would say social graces is a must have. Whether you are the kid on the playground, the parent in child pick-up line, or the person in the corner office, social etiquette can be a gamechanger in how you are perceived and received. The best way to get along and interact with others is by practicing social graces. You can be talented in a lot of areas or possess special skills, but without social graces you will only go so far. If your character, or who you show up as is outside social norms or causes others to be uncomfortable in your presence, you are limited in terms of positive effectiveness. A pastor I know would say it this way, "Your talent can take you to the top, but it's your character that keeps you there." Etiquette speaks to character and how you show up to represent yourself and others.

You mentioned dining skills as a business opportunity. What were you referencing?

Sometimes job interviews are conducted over a luncheon or evening meal. Too, though an interview may not be officially announced, potential employers are almost always observant when engaging you with you over a meal. Be always mindful of this point. Potential employers are watching you to see how you conduct yourself. They want to know if you are the type of person they can trust to entertain a client if the opportunity presents itself. In such cases, others may take notice of how you handle utensils, how you chew your food or the pace of eating, or they may observe your mannerism when conversing with the waitress. Both verbal and nonverbal skills are important. There are many unspoken rules when it comes to dining during a business or professional exchange. It's not like the etiquette police will throw you in jail for not recognizing certain protocol, but you may be judged or viewed negatively because of it. Knowing and observing dining skills etiquette gets you one step closer to the next promotion. You can raise the bar on social elegance and acceptance by knowing proper dining skills.

ʙᴀsɪᴄ ᴛᴇʀᴍs ᴛᴏ ᴋɴᴏᴡ

Renita Jackson

A la Carte

A la carte is a French word, which refers to the food items listed on the menu. Each item is listed, ordered and price separately. You choose one or more items to make your meal.

Appetizers

Hors d'oeuvres, canapé and crudités are all fancy ways to say finger foods. They are delicious bite sized foods that are usually served at happy hours, receptions or before a main meal. At some parties and networking events, they are the only foods served. However, just because they are casual foods that you may possibly eat with your fingers, this is no reason to throw your manners out the door. Here are some tips to remember when dining on such foods:

- Use your fingers not your hands to eat the foods. Using a fork is always an acceptable alternative.

- Always use a plate to hold or rest your food and a napkin to keep hands clean.

- Don't overcrowd your plate with a lot of food.

- Use a utensil, if available, to pick up food from the serving tray to avoid touching and contaminating other foods.

- Take the food items closest to you to avoid reaching over the other food. Be mindful of dangling jewelry and sleeves when reaching for you selections.

- Don't double dip, no one wants to share your food with you.

- Don't eat while standing over the food table. Select your food choices and step away.

- Use a clean plate if you return for more food.

Body Language

Body language is a conscious and sometimes unconscious communication. Gestures, facial expressions, eye movement, exposure and physical contact are also powerful forms of silent speaking.

- Arms crossed – a sign of defensiveness or disagreement

- Tugging or playing with your hair – a sign of thinking or concentration

- Stroking a mustache or beard – a sign of thinking or concentration

- Drumming fingers or tapping your feet – a sign of growing impatient

- Head tilting – a sign of disbelief

- Raised eyebrows – a sign of disbelief or ready to debate

- Picking or biting fingernails – a sign of nervousness or insecurity

- Cheek placed in hand – a sign of concentration or confusion

- Fidgeting – a sign of boredom

- Touching all fingertips together in a peak position – a sign of control or authority

- Clicking pens – a sign of boredom

- Fingertips to forehead – a sign of thinking

- Pulling of the ear lobe – a sign you are attempting to decide or you're Carol Burnette!

- Sitting, standing, and walking up straight – a sign of confidence!

Business Card

A business card is a small card providing information about a business or business representative. The business card should tell people who you are, what you do and how to reach you. It is also your calling card and forwarding agent that can be attached to a gift, report, information, etc. It should reflect you or who you represent.

In this day of technology many people prefer to exchange contact by making a quick entry with electronic business cards, or direct entry into their smartphones and use of Quick Response (QR) codes).

Buffet Dining

Buffet style dining is a convenient way to accommodate a party of several people in place of a more formal sit-down dinner.

When setting up a buffet-style meal, the table should start with the plates and end with the utensils and napkins. This way, guests do not have to manage balancing a plate, utensils, and napkins while trying to place food on their plate.

Utensils should be used to put food onto your plate. If you return to the buffet line for additional food, always use a clean plate.

Correspondence

Correspondence is an exchange of information by way of written, typed or data entry communication. Common correspondences include, but not limited to business and personal letters, thank you notes and greeting cards. Written communication is a valuable skill which is appreciated by the recipient. The time taken to compose and send a written thank you note can add volumes of value to your character.

Excuse Me

This is one of the proper words that should be used in an apologetic plea. Be careful to say, "Excuse me" and not the abbreviate "scuse me", that so many people tend to say.

Eye Contact

Eye contact during introductions, speaking and conversation is vital. It shows attentiveness, interest and possibly concern in what is being said. It also shows respect and sincerity to the person with whom the conversation or talk is shared. Keep as much eye contact as possible with the person or persons you are in engaging with. It not only shows good manners, but it also shows self-confidence.

Host/Hostess

The person who is generally responsible for welcoming customers first as they enter a food service facility, seating them and alerting the server of their presence.

A host/hostess can also be the person who has extended an invitation to join them in their home, restaurant, or function where they have planned a meeting, dining, or entertainment.

Host is typically associated with male and hostess with females.

Hostess Gifts

Hostess gifts are given to the host/hostess of a party, event, or occasion in which they have invited you to partake in. It is a kind gesture of thankfulness for the invitation. It is still in good taste to send a written thank you note to the host/hostess after the event has passed.

Networking

See chapter on Networking: The Ultimate Power Tool

Place Cards

Place cards are used at dining functions denoting where the named guest is supposed to sit at the table. Cards should not be moved to another location by the guests.

Place Settings

The order or way the dishes, utensils and glassware are arranged on the table for formal dining.

Formal Table Setting

- White wine glass
- Bread knife
- Dessert spoon
- Water glass
- Cup and saucer (place on table with dessert)
- Cake fork
- Bread plate
- Red wine glass
- Place card
- Napkin
- Salad fork
- Fork
- Serving plate
- Dinner knife
- Salad knife
- Teaspoon
- Soup spoon

QR Codes

A "Quick Response Code" A type of barcode or a matrix pattern of black and white squares, typically used for storing URLs or other information which can be read by a digital device, such as a camera on a smartphone.

RSVP

R.S.V.P. is an abbreviation for the French word *Repondez s'il vous plait,* which means, *"Respond if you please" or reply.* If you receive an invitation with R.S.V.P. on it, you are to contact the sender of the invitation and let them know whether or not you plan to attend the function they have invited you to. You should respond as soon as possible, but most definitely prior to the date provided next to the RSVP. If no date is provided, respond as soon as possible. Remember, *RSVP-ASAP!*

If you are sending an invitation, the *RSVP* will help you in planning for the number of people that will attend your event.

An invitation that has the words *"regrets only"* means you need to reply only if you are unable to attend the event.

Don't assume that the person sending you an invite will know whether or not you will attend their function just because you are very close friends. No matter how close the friendship or relation, rsvp!

Thank You Notes

If someone takes the time to do something for you or give you something, you should take the time to properly thank them by sending a handwritten *thank you* note. It's more personal and more appreciated than an electronic message. Thank you notes should be sent after job interviews and when someone gives you a lead or referral.

Handwritten thank you notes are best. Avoid using thank you notes with pre-printed messages inside. Avoid using email responses as your primary source for a thank you note. If you do send an email thank you, follow up with a written note as well. Send the thank you note in 24 hours or as soon as possible.

Tipping

Tipping is a way of showing your appreciation of the service you have received from someone. A tip can speak louder than words. Was the service remarkable, tolerable, or very unacceptable? Even though tipping is a voluntary gesture, make it a practice to tip anyone who renders you a service. . . it's the polite thing to do.

However, if personal service is provided to you, tipping is appropriate. If you are not sure if you should tip someone, just do it. It's better to error on the side of tipping someone than not tipping. When in doubt, tip.

The amount of your tip should show your appreciation of the services rendered. The customary tip is 15% to 20% of the bill before taxes. Be sure to review your bill carefully as some dining establishments automatically include a gratuity on their tickets. You are not required to add an additional tip if the gratuity has already been added. If the service was not to your expectations, you still need to supply a tip. If the service is poor, consider a 10% tip and possibly a simple explanation of what you were displeased with. If the service was very poor, consider discussing your dissatisfaction with the management. Remember, service and product are two different things. If you are in a restaurant and your meal is not to your satisfaction, this should not reflect in the tips of the waiter/waitress, who may have had nothing to do with the food preparation. Tips can vary from region to region. Take your local into consideration when tipping.

Toast

Toasting is a celebratory announcement normally done during special occasions and celebrations. The toaster should get the attention of guests (not by banging the glass with a knife or other utensil), make the toast announce-ment, raise their glass to drink, and invite others to raise their glass the same. Try to avoid clicking glasses during the toast. The guest of honor or "toastee" should not drink to the toast dedicated to them.

COMPILED BY

Dr. Larthenia Howard

Dr. Larthenia Howard is a two-time award-winning author and creator of the *How to Write a Book in 31 Days System©*—a step-by-step process that shows aspiring authors how to create value-add content that attracts visibility and expands influence. In her more recently developed course, *From a Book to a Business©*, she teaches authors how to create multiple streams of income from a book, and grow a business beyond the pages.

Larthenia has been featured on TBN Network, The Lee Pitts Show, National Association of Secondary School Principals periodical, Professional Women Network platform, and national and local syndicated broadcasts. She is host of the Dr. Empowerment Blog Talk Radio Show and certified as a Neuro-Linguistic Programming (NLP) Master Practitioner and Emotional Intelligence Facilitator.

Prior to becoming an author and entrepreneur, Dr. Howard served as an English teacher, professor, and as a member of the National No Child Left Behind Task Force in Washington, D.C., where she was instrumental in legislative recommendations for education reform.

Five Fun Facts About Larthenia:

- A skateboarder, or as she says, "A lover of Land Yachts"
- Enjoys exploration in caves around the world
- Rocks out to country and 70's/80's pop music
- Takes acoustic guitar playing lessons
- Goes bananas for a Wood Wick candle